THE MORAL MANDATE TO VOTE

God's Priorities in Government

by

Kenneth M. Wilson, M.D.

HUNTINGTON HOUSE PUBLISHERS

Huntington House Publishers
P.O. Box 53788
Lafayette, Louisiana 70505

PRINTED IN THE UNITED STATES OF AMERICA

Library of Congress Card Catalog Number 00-103970
ISBN 1-56384-177-0

Contents

Appendices

Acknowledgments

LeLynn Wilson, my faithful and wonderful wife, for her love in struggling with me through these ideas in Scripture, in prayer, and in relationships; Rachael, Brent, Stephen, and Lisa Wilson, my precious children, for being patient with me as I struggled with God, myself, and others to understand and articulate His truth; My parents, for raising me in an environment where I could learn God's truth; Marion Duckworth, for her invaluable editing, prayer, and encouragement; Lael Arrington, speaker and author, for recognizing God's divine appointment to encourage me to pursue this book, and doing it so well; Michael Howden, Executive Director of Oregon Family Research Council, friend and godly man of grace and truth for his example and encouragement; Tim Gilmer, friend, for being open to God's truth and coming alongside at a critical time—with excellent suggestions; Cam and Susan Buck, friends who continued to believe in me when it was not easy; Steve and Krysti Emerson, good friends, for beginning this journey with me; Chuck Colson, for developing crucial and effective ministries based on a biblical worldview; and leading us misguided Christians back to a biblical worldview; Dr. David Anderson, pastor and professor who taught me to really study the Bible; Russell Wilson, Esquire, my brother and friend, a great attorney, husband and father; Ron Norquist, for helping me to see the leaks in my thinking that needed to be plugged; Randy Alcorn, for courageously leading the charge before most of us understood how insidiously abortion continues to undermine our society; The many who have gone before me to convey God's truth on these issues; Two sincere women and six sincere men whom I love, for being used by God to compel me to write this book.

"The care of human life and happiness
and not their destruction is the first
and only legitimate object of good government."

—Thomas Jefferson

Introduction

What author would ever place both religion and politics in the same book?

Only a masochist would discuss both topics simultaneously! Don't we have enough controversy already? The reason I've tackled both is important; we will all stand before God one day to give an account for our actions here on earth. That includes how we vote. Most people already have an opinion on abortion and euthanasia. We have apparently settled down comfortably with our chosen viewpoints. But there are still many questions that need answers, including:

- Is there a right and wrong way to vote?
- Even if I vote in a wrong way, won't God forgive me?
- Isn't voting part of politics—and isn't the Church supposed to avoid that subject?
- How can abortion be wrong if I believe the fetus is only a potential person—not a complete one?
- A woman has the right to choose to control her own body. Isn't that a personal decision?
- Should I determine how to mark my ballot based *only* on pro-choice or pro-life issues?
- Surely God thinks that euthanasia and physician-assisted suicide are legitimate ways to avoid painful suffering. He doesn't want us to suffer, does He?
- I am personally against abortion, but, isn't it best to allow others the freedom to choose?

The answers to these questions will determine the future of America. I would suggest that there is too much at stake to place this relentless debate on the back burner. Pro-choice advocates risk losing far more than their freedom to choose. Pro-life advocates risk far more than the lives of millions of fetuses. I believe that both viewpoints are inadequate.

In the pages that follow, we'll find biblical answers to these questions and, in the process, gain the tools to change the course of history. Our future—immediate and eternal—depend upon it.

1.

The Beginnings of New Thought

Does God care about the way I vote?

Until last year, I did not think about voting as a spiritual issue. Then one evening, I began a discussion with a Christian woman who is very involved in the Church. When she found out that I was voting for a certain candidate, she expressed her surprise. A more compassionate way to vote, she told me, was for a different candidate. To vote for the alternate candidate was "more Christian" because of the benefits to the poor, the elderly, the environment, and other important issues.

I agreed with her that compassionate love in action is important. In fact, I mentioned many charitable organizations that my wife and I support financially. Some of these include programs that give food to hungry children, shelter the homeless and battered women, and give Christmas gifts to children of prisoners.

Questions, Questions

Following that discussion, I asked myself: "How could two Christians who are both active in the Church, who love God, and desire to do what's right, come to different conclusions about the correct way to vote?

That led to other questions like the ones I posed in the introduction.

• Is the way I vote really important to God?

• Does the Lordship of Jesus Christ in my life extend even to the way I vote?

• How important are the issues she mentioned in comparison to the issues of abortion and euthanasia?

• Could the way a Christian votes ever be a sin?

For one year, I searched to find acceptable answers. Being an intense person, I agonized over the Scriptures, read countless books, talked with numerous Christian leaders, applied logic and prayed continuously, crying out to God. Some Christian leaders told me that voting was purely political; voting could never be a sin. I did not have a reasoned argument to answer them, yet I felt in my heart that voting really could be a sin.

Finally answers began to come, but they did not come easily. There were no good resources to explain to me how God might vote or why. When I ultimately arrived at an acceptable answer, many people whom I respected did not agree. In the midst of this struggle, I asked God to release me from the responsibility of being the lone voice in my circle of friends–taking a verbal and literal stand.

God answered, "*NO!*"

Standing alone would be difficult for me. Like most of you, I enjoy being appreciated and liked. So, I argued with God.

Difficult Answers

Perhaps you can relate to my experience. I felt as though I was standing in the eye of a hurricane. In the restful calm on the beach, I could defiantly spit long distances into the gentle ocean waves. A breeze played on my face and I felt good about my success for quite a while.

God is patient. However, the calm in the eye of the storm inevitably yielded to the hurricane winds and gigantic waves. I soon realized that no matter which way I turned in this matter, I was in *serious* trouble. No one can escape from God.

As a result, I now pray differently. Instead of asking to escape from God's plan, I pray that God will use my difficult struggle in search of truth. May He use my experiences to help others in His Church.

Fighting Fear

Perhaps we have been too complacent with our pat answers to the question of voting on abortion. Over twenty years ago, the magazine *Moody Monthly* lamented the silence of the evangelical Church: "Evangelicalism as a whole has uttered no real outcry. We've organized no protest. Do we need more time to think abortion through? Isn't seven years long enough?"[1]

Although some demonstrations and marches have occurred, the Church, with a few exceptions, has remained on the sidelines. After twenty years, has anything changed? Has the Prince of this world spiritually blinded us Christians? Are we afraid of searching for the truth about abortion and euthanasia? Do we fear the possible consequences?

I believe that much of the problem in the Church over social (political) issues, especially abortion and euthanasia, has been due to fear. Some of these fears are valid—others are not. But, it often seems that emotions do factor heavily into the decision-making process, rather than depending upon reasoned dialogue from the Scriptures.

Congressman Henry Hyde has been a staunch defender of human life for decades. As he has attempted to convince people of the truth about abortion, he has come to the realization that, "You cannot change someone's mind by using reason when they did not use reason to arrive at their decision."[2]

He's right. Fear and opinions, without diligent research, may be the way many Christians have formed their conclusions—even some in leadership positions.

I eventually discovered that many Christian leaders such as Billy Graham, Pope John Paul II, R.C. Sproul, and Chuck Colson believe that voting was a Christian duty and subject to the Lordship of Christ. I also found out that taking a stand on abortion—especially voting on abortion—can be a frightening and lonely experience. It was for me.

Relationships were strained near the breaking point. Only a Godly love held them together. It was intimidating when good people whom I respected, told me that I was wrong. But their arguments were neither Scriptural nor logical. I wondered—could these leaders have been intimidated or influenced by other people?

Our reluctance to take a stand as Christians reminds me of a day when our family was eating lunch and looking out on the green pastures of our small farm. Eight cute little baby lambs, whose combined weight was less than one hundred pounds, were frolicking playfully.

They came racing toward a mother cow that was grazing—fourteen hundred pounds of automatic lawnmower. As the lambs raced full speed to within six feet of her, the mother cow jumped back in fear and trotted off. We all laughed at the absurdity of such a large animal with such power being frightened by baby lambs.

Sometimes we in the Church act like the cow. We are afraid of the many who fight against us from the outside or the inside. Yet, because of God's power, His Church stands stronger than a million armies. The Church in Germany allowed Hitler to kill millions because it was afraid—it did not need to happen.

For in His Holy Scriptures, God says that we need not fear people.

Jesus said, "Let not your heart be troubled, neither be afraid" (John 14:27).

Solomon writes, "The fear of man brings a snare" (Prov. 29:25).

David was a man with a very good reason to be afraid. After all, an entire army was chasing him with murder on their minds! Yet he wrote, "The Lord is the strength of my life, of whom shall I be afraid?" (Ps. 27:1).

Besides fear of other people, we also tend to be afraid of potential division within the Church. This parody of an old Latin hymn says:

> The strife is o'er, the battle done;
> The church has split, and our side won.[3]

A Church split is a legitimate fear because nobody wins. But friction doesn't have to lead to fracture. Caring and confronting are not opposites.

> Care-fronting unifies concern for relationship with concerns for goals . . .

> Care-fronting is the way to communicate with both impact and respect, with truth and love. . . .

> I love you—If I love you I must tell you the truth

> I want your love—I want your truth

> Love me enough to tell me the truth.[4]

We must ask ourselves: Is this truth important enough to risk friction in the Church? Is the killing of thirty-eight million fetuses in the past twenty-seven years important enough to confront our fears?

Conclusions

We Christians need to ask ourselves new questions and arrive at informed answers when it comes to the sanctity of life. We need to know how God views voting on the issues of abortion and euthanasia: Arguing with God is self-defeating. He doesn't want us to allow the fear of people, or potential divisions in the Church to stop us. Instead, God calls us to speak and act out His truth in love—care-fronting. As we shall see, that has always been our responsibility.

Notes

1. Sweening, G., Ed., "Whatever happened to the Evangelical?" *Moody Monthly* (May 1980): 21.

2. Hyde, Henry, *Speech for Oregon Right to Life*, Lake Oswego, Oregon, 6 November 1999.

3. Fowler, P., *Abortion—Toward an Evangelical Consensus* (Portland, OR: Multnomah Press, 1987), 13.

4. Augsburger, D., *Caring Enough to Confront* (Ventura, CA: Regal Books, 1973), 8-12.

True Religion Is Compassion

Abortion is now the most common surgical procedure in America.[1] One out of every four babies conceived in America is killed by abortion.[2] Over 95 percent of these abortions are performed for the convenience of the mother.[3]

The Alan Guttmacher Institute, a pro-abortion research group, states the most common reason given by a woman for having an abortion: "Three out of four said that a baby would interfere with work, school, or other responsibilities."[4] The good news is that abortions are becoming less frequent. Among teenagers, the number has slowly decreased for the past several years. The latest official statistics available from the Center for Disease Control (CDC) are from 1997.

> The number of abortions for every 1,000 live births dropped from 314 in 1996 to 305 in 1997—also the lowest since 1975, the CDC said. . . . The CDC cited several factors for the decline, including reduced access to abortion, an increased willingness to use contraception, and possibly different attitudes about the moral implications of abortion.[5]

The Church in Spiritual Isolation

The question arises immediately: Should Christians be involved in political issues like this?

Political activism is not the mission of Christ's Church—neither is spiritual isolationism. These two extremes are rampant in American churches today. In what follows, a balanced alternative to these two extreme attitudes will be presented.

Over the past century, liberal theologians have gutted the Holy Scriptures of objective spiritual truth. Spiritual isolationism has been the evangelical church's response to this Neo-Orthodox social gospel. Devoid of the foundation of God's revealed truth, the liberal theologians substituted social help programs as the gospel. This was a forerunner of postmodern thought. The evangelical church, in an effort to save truth, has overreacted by declaring that only what is spiritual in the realm of heaven is important. According to this view, the gospel refers *only* to spiritual salvation. Fortunately, the Catholic church has continued to maintain an emphasis on practical social compassion as the expression of Christ's love.

Many spiritual leaders have proclaimed the importance of this compassionate outworking of Christ's love. In his book, *Storm Warning,* Billy Graham asks us to become involved in our societal issues.

> Are there things that you can do to express your concern and be of help while continuing to stand for traditional Christian values? Yes, I believe there is, and I believe it is our Christian duty to do something. To begin with, it would help to be informed on these issues. . . . The second thing you can do is to learn more about the organizations that educate, inform, and assist men and women on these issues. Your pastor may be able to point you to responsible national or local organizations that focus on these concerns. Third, you can volunteer to help your church, civic organization, or local special-interest group.[6]

Operating from a biblical worldview, Chuck Colson has helped direct the evangelical church back to the truth of compassionate action with his many programs to help prisoners, their families, and communities.

> . . . The Lord's cultural commission is inseparable from the great commission. That may be a jarring statement for many conservative Christians, who, through much of the twentieth century, have shunned the notion of reforming culture, associating that concept with the liberal social gospel. The only task of the church, many fundamentalists and evangelicals have believed, is to save as many lost souls

as possible from a world literally going to hell. But, this implicit denial of a Christian worldview is unbiblical and is the reason we have lost so much of our influence in the world. Salvation does not consist simply of freedom from sin; salvation also means being restored to the task we were given in the beginning—the job of creating culture.[7]

Major portions of God's Word in both the Old and New Testaments command us to care for the needs of the poor and helpless. All of them command social action or works to accompany our belief. One example is James 1:27: "*True religion and undefiled before God and the Father is this: to help the widows and orphans in their suffering and to keep yourself unstained from the world*" (emphasis mine).

Providing the physical needs of food and clothing for the poor proves a mature faith. So the Bible agrees with a *total* gospel—not spiritually isolated thinking. Since compassion for pregnant teenagers and abortions both require physical needs to be met, shouldn't the Church be involved in these issues?

Faith and Works

It's popular for people to quote James 2:17 when they want to prove that good works are an essential ingredient of faith: "Faith without works is dead." However, many of these same people conveniently omit the previous verses. These are the good works that James declares to be essential: caring for the physical needs of the poor, widows, and orphans (1:28, 2:15-16). *Physical care* is true religion.

Through James, God confronts our spiritually isolated view of Christianity.

> What does it profit, brothers, though a man says he has faith, and has no works? Can faith save him? (no) If a brother or sister is naked and destitute of daily food, and one of you says to them "Go in peace, be warm and be filled." Yet, you do not give them those things which are needed for the body, what profit is there? Even so, faith if it does not have works is dead, being alone. (James 2:14-20)

Dr. David Livingston was a medical doctor whose life exemplified James's teaching. As a physician, I can relate to his passion to reach people. In his case, it was Africans. He preached the good news of Jesus Christ while helping those in physical need.

> My great object was to be like Him—to imitate Him as far as He could be imitated. We have not the power of working miracles, but we can do a little in the way of healing the sick, and I sought a medical education in order that I might be like Him. . . . A woman's criticism of his concern with trade, as if that had nothing to do with Christ—drew this fiery response: Nowhere have I appeared as anything but a servant of God, who has simply followed the leading of His hand. My views of what is missionary duty are not so contracted as those whose ideal is a dumpy sort of man with a Bible under his arm. I have labored in bricks and mortar, at the forge and carpenter's bench, as well as preaching. . . .[8]

Perhaps the most recent famous example of such a commitment to the whole gospel is Mother Teresa of Calcutta. Her courageous example of helping the poor and needy of India has inspired innumerable young people to commit their lives to serving God in this same way. This Catholic nun's death was a great loss for the world.

To God, true religion is compassionate care of those around us who are in need. The Bible, great Christian leaders, and common sense all tell us that this is the right answer.

Where Is Our Compassion?

At this point, I must warn you that I may step on a few toes. Consider the average local church budget. What percentage goes to the poor and helpless? Embarrassingly, our use—or abuse—of money often proves that buildings and programs are more important to us.

There's nothing wrong with buildings and programs. But are we spending more money on ourselves "in the name of God" than we spend on the needy? The passage in James asks if it profits us to teach correct doctrine and "love others" but fail to demonstrate Christ in action? Has Jesus' command to "love thy neighbor as thyself" been reduced and isolated to telling the gospel?

Shortly after beginning to struggle with these issues, I wrote an essay asking the question: "I wonder what would happen if?" I visualized a group of Christians in a local church who learned that their money offering to God would all go to help others rather than keeping it for buildings and programs. I concluded that people would give more.

Well, God was listening; and, this time He answered, "YES!" Leaders in my church announced that the upcoming "Thanksgiving Miracle" offering to thank God for the blessings of the year, would all be given to relief efforts. Some would go for food and supplies in foreign countries. The remainder would be sent to Sudan for helping Christians who had been captured and sold into slavery by Muslim soldiers. I wept.

That following week, the offering was enormous—way over anything that had ever been given. I cried again.

The unbelieving world recognizes that a genuine Christianity must meet people where they are, and that includes their social needs. They can point to Jesus, who spent a lot of time healing people physically. That was part of His *Good News* that God loved them. Hurting people matter to God.

The Washington Post exclaimed the success of 260 churches in Ottawa County, Michigan who exemplified this principle.[9] They helped people find jobs, gave emotional support, friendship, and financial instruction. In October 1997, every able-bodied welfare recipient in the county was employed. All 220,000 in the county had a job. Churches were helping people in need. Isn't it likely that those who experienced this practical help were more ready to listen to the good news that God loved them?

We Christians cannot allow fear to stop us from doing what is morally right—we cannot hide in spiritual isolationism. Instead, we must tell about the grace of God in salvation and demonstrate the love of God in action—faith and works.

We are to obey God's commands to love others by meeting their physical as well as spiritual needs.

How does all of this relate to the unborn?

Most people agree that the fetus is a human, scientifically speaking. But is it a fully developed "person?" Is that how God views it? If He sees it as less than a person, then we Christians need not be concerned about thirty-eight million deaths. If, however, God does view the fetus as a person, then that fetus (he or she) is eligible to receive, from us, the *whole* gospel of love.

Conclusions

Abortion is the most common surgical procedure in America. Our response as God's Church should avoid the extreme views of political zealots and spiritual isolationists. God calls us to demonstrate our faith with compassionate works.

Leading Christians have both taught and exemplified that balance. These compassionate works include helping people physically.

In the next chapter, we will examine the question of whether the fetus is a fully developed "person." If it is, then God expects us to give him or her the *whole* gospel of love.

"Let me give you one definition of ethics:
It is good to maintain life and to further life;
it is bad to damage and destroy life.
And this ethic, profound, universal, has the
significance of a religion.
It is religion."

—Dr. Albert Schweitzer
Nobel Prize Winner, *Religion*

Notes

1. National Center for Health Statistics, Atlanta, GA, 1997.

2. Facts in Brief: Induced Abortion (Alan Guttmacher Institute, 1998): 1. Also accessed 19 February 2000; available from http:// www.agiusa.org/pubs/fb_induced_abortion. html, revised 2/2000.

3. U.S. Department of Health and Human Services, Center for Disease Control, 1997.

4. Facts in Brief, 1.

5. The Associated Press, "Abortions fall in '97 to lowest since 1978," *The Oregonian,* 7 January 2000, A1.

6. Graham, B., *Storm Warning* (Dallas: Word Publishing, 1992), 240-241.

7. Colson, C., and Nancy Pearcy, *How Now Shall We Live* (Wheaton, IL: Tyndale House Publishers, 1999), 295-296.

8. Wellman, S., *David Livingston-Missionary and Explorer* (Uhrichsville, OH: Barbour Publishing), 167-168.

9. Peter, J., "Michigan County Finds Jobs for All Welfare Recipients," *The Washington Post,* 16 September 1997, A05.

Fetology:
Medical Science and the Bible

I was taught in medical school that the beginning of human life is conception. This is basic embryology. When the sperm fertilizes the egg, a unique human life begins that has never before existed. The life is human by definition. The forty-six human chromosomes are a living entity that is genetically different from both the father and the mother—it is unique. It is not merely part of the mother's body any more than it is a part of the father's body. It is temporarily living inside the mother. There is no controversy about this fact from medical textbooks or physicians.

Medical Documentation

Dr. Hymie Gordon, a professor of medical genetics at Mayo Clinic in 1981, testified to this fact in a U.S. Senate hearing:

> But now we can say, unequivocally, that the question of when human life begins is no longer a question for theological or philosophical dispute. It is an established scientific fact. Theologians and philosophers may go on to debate the meaning of life or the purpose of life, but it is an established fact that all life, including human life, begins at the moment of conception.[1]

Dr. Cunningham, an Obstetrics-Gynecologist, wrote a textbook on his specialty. In it, he declared, "The status of the fetus has been elevated to that of a patient who, in large measure, can be given the same meticulous care that obstetricians have long given the pregnant woman."[2] Even official government documents acknowledge this fact.

According to the report by the subcommittee to the U.S. Senate Judiciary Committee in 1981, S-158, 97th Congress, 1st session:

> Physicians, biologists, and other scientists agree that conception marks the beginning of the life of a human being— a being that is alive and is a member of the human species. There is overwhelming agreement on this point in countless medical, biological, and scientific writings.

This document listed thirteen medical textbooks defining conception as the beginning of individual life. Even at the time of the *Roe v. Wade* decision, there was overwhelming evidence of this fact. In 1989, the U.S. Supreme Court let stand a Missouri statute that stated that conception is the beginning of human life.[3]

There is no argument about the medical facts. Abortion does kill a living human being. But we must answer the question of whether that human is a fully developed person who is worthy of protection, or merely a potential person.

The Hippocratic Oath of Physicians

The Hippocratic Oath has been the physician's vow for at least twenty-four hundred years. Although I did not swear to Apollo and Aesculapius (or the gods and goddesses), I did recite that oath along with all of my colleagues during medical school graduation ceremonies. Part of this oath directs that you will not knowingly give a pregnant woman anything that will cause her to have an abortion.

"I will give no deadly medicine to any one if asked, nor suggest such counsel; and, *in like manner* I will not give a woman a pessary to produce abortion."[4]

So as early as 400 B.C., human life was valued by even pagan Greek physicians. To kill a child in the womb was to kill a person. This is evidenced by the phrase "in like manner." The deadly medicine of the pessary did not kill the woman—it killed the fetus.

This refusal to abort was an essential core of the Hippocratic Oath: physicians were to do no harm to *anyone*. Physicians today who perform abortions violate this oath; they kill a human being. That fetal human being has been recognized as someone. The fetus has been recognized as a person for at least twenty-four hundred years.

There is evidence that physicians still consider the fetus to be a human person. Today, surgeons perform operations to correct abnormalities on the fetuses as early as twenty-one weeks gestation.[5] Tiny patients with spina bifida and other serious defects receive care inside the womb. After a Caesarian section, the baby is brought outside the womb with the umbilical cord still attached. The operation is performed. The baby is then placed back into the uterus and the womb closed.

Does God Have an Opinion?

Although a few doctors I know may believe otherwise, they definitely are not God. There is a surgeon I know who loves to answer the telephone in the doctors' hospital lounge: "Doctor's Lounge, God speaking." I keep expecting a Voice from heaven, saying, "This is *not* my beloved Son; I am *not* well-pleased."

Psalms 139:13-16, Jeremiah 1:5, Judges 13:7, Luke 1:41,44, and Exodus 21:22-25 all point to God's view of the unborn as human beings and persons. But most amazing of all is the fact that God did not send our Savior, Jesus Christ, into the world as an adult. God the Father chose to send His only born Son as a fetus: Jesus, the fetus. That is what the angel Gabriel announced to the Virgin Mary in Matthew 1:23: "Behold the virgin shall be with child *(pregnant)*, and bear *(deliver)* a Son, and they shall call His name Immanuel, which is translated, God with us."

Fortunately, Jesus the fetus was born into a Jewish culture where abortion was not legal. These people feared God and honored His creative act. (They had only one word for both a fetus and newborn—*yeled*.) Such a fetal incarnation act by God is a strong statement about the value of the unborn. But there is even stronger evidence for the personhood of the fetus.

Examples of Fetal Persons (with Potential)

Samson was separated to serve God as a Nazarite while he was still in his mother's womb. Judges 13:7 declares,

"You will conceive and have a son. Now do not drink any wine or strong drink. Do not eat anything unclean. Because, the child will be a Nazarite to God from the *womb* to the day of his death."

The angel of the Lord instructed the mother of Samson not to contaminate the unborn child's body inside her womb. Why? Because the unborn child was already separated to serve God. Any violation of the Nazarite vow by his mother's eating or drinking would pass on prohibited elements to the child's body, thereby violating Samson's Nazarite separation to God. (Quite a medical insight by God into embryological nutrition.) God views the fetus as a person, not merely a potential person.

The prophet Jeremiah had a similar fetal separation to God as a person. Jeremiah 1:5 says, "Before I formed you in the womb I knew you; and, before you came out of the womb I set you apart and ordained you as a prophet to the nations." God not only formed and knew Jeremiah before he was born, God also had a plan for him as a fetal human being. Unborn children are designed and known by God. Unborn fetuses already have a purpose in God's plan.

John the Baptist was a fetal human capable of responding to spiritual phenomenon in Luke 1:15, 41, and 44:

> For he will be great in the sight of the Lord, and shall drink neither wine nor strong drink. He will also be filled with the Holy Spirit, even from his mother's womb. . . . And it happened, when Elizabeth heard the greeting of Mary, that the babe leaped in her womb. . . . For indeed, as soon as the voice of your greeting sounded in my ears, the babe leaped in my womb for joy.

The fetal John, inside Elizabeth, was responding to Mary's voice. John responded to the mother of Jesus who was carrying the fetal Jesus in her womb. This spiritual response would require the Holy Spirit to fill John inside Elizabeth's womb. This is exactly what was predicted and announced by the angel to Elizabeth concerning her son, John, that "he will be filled with the Holy Spirit, even from his mother's womb."

In addition, the Greek word *brephos* is usually translated "newborn or child." But in Luke 1:41 and 44, this word is used of John the Baptist as he leaps in the womb of his mother. King David tells us about his fetal experience in Psalms 139:13-16:

> For You formed my inward parts; You wove me in my mother's womb. I will give thanks to You, for I am fearfully and wonderfully made. . . . My frame was not hidden from You, when I was made in secret, and skillfully wrought in the depths of the earth; Your eyes have seen my unformed substance; and in Your book were all written the days that were ordained for me, when as yet there was not one of them. (NASB)

God designs human fetuses. God views them as persons capable of spiritual response and service to Him. To God, fetuses are not merely potential persons.

The "Potential" Controversy

I believe that this is one of the most crucial yet misunderstood aspects of the abortion debate. Even though I didn't give much thought to abortion for many years as a Christian, I realized as a medical doctor that the fetus was a living human being. I believed that it was wrong to kill this human being, as declared in the Hippocratic Oath. But it was only when I saw God's view of this fetus, as a full human person, that I became active in the abortion debate.

Perhaps if I had been thinking more logically, I would have realized the logical fallacy in my thinking. By using the term "potential person," I was placing an arbitrary judgment on the value of that human. When does the potential person become a complete or "actual" person? Have I reached *my* full potential as a person?

What criteria do we use to determine the precise moment at which the change occurs from "potential" to "actual"? Physical development, intellectual capacity, the ability to interact with others, and self-awareness have all been suggested as potential criteria. But these arbitrary criteria raise serious problems.

Dr. Peter Singer, Professor of Bioethics at Princeton University, has no problem killing children after they are born. He stated that one month *after* birth would be sufficient time to see if a newborn human should be allowed to qualify as a person.[6]

Physical development is a particularly dangerous criterion. The brain of a newborn baby is not fully developed until at least *one year* after birth. The process of myelinization continues outside the womb to complete the development of the brain. (Myelinization is similar to the plastic coating on an electrical wire.) Severe mental and developmental retardation are inevitable without it. A dog or cat would be more intelligent and physically adept than a human being if the process were to stop before one year. So, do we wait for *complete* physical development before granting complete human status?

Speaking of animals, intellectual capacity is also a dangerous criterion. What about children who are born with mental retardation? Their intellectual capacity is often less than some animals. Do we set a standard IQ below which we deny acceptance into personhood? In Hitler's Germany, twelve million people eventually died as evidence of the disastrous effects of this kind of criterion.

The ability to interact meaningfully with others appears to be a promising criterion. But what about our elderly parents with severe dementia or Alzheimer's Disease? Do we remove our parents from the roster of persons when they no longer interact? Have they reverted to potential personhood? Should it surprise us that Dr. Singer also advocates the killing of incompetent persons *of any age* if their families decide their lives are "not worth living?"[7]

Self-awareness is another potential criterion. What about the person in a coma? Is he or she self-aware? How do we know? Is electrical activity in the brain an absolute criterion for self-awareness? By answering *yes*, do we not side with the physical reductionists who claim that mankind is the sum total of the physical parts, devoid of anything spiritual? [8]

The Worst Potential I'd Ever Seen

I was completing my rotation through pediatrics in medical school. One night, the professor escorted me to the pediatric intensive care unit to care for a patient. As I looked into the bassinet, I saw a perfectly formed newborn girl—all except for one part. She did not have a brain.

I had never seen an anencephalic child except in textbook pictures. Every few moments, she would stop breathing. No heroic measures were being used—after all, she had no brain. But for some reason, I was assigned to gently touch her every few minutes to stimulate breathing.

To be honest, I was angry. I had worked twelve hours that day, I was going to be up all night, and I had to begin another twelve hours in the morning. What possible purpose could it serve to spend all night touching a little girl without a brain? Why did it have to be me? God often works in subtle ways; this night was my night. I had plenty of time to think—hour after hour. As I questioned this futile assignment, scripture verses like Exodus 4:11 came to mind, where Moses also questioned God at the burning bush. "And the Lord said unto him, "Who has made man's mouth? Or who makes the dumb, or deaf, or the seeing, or the blind? Have not I the Lord?"

My heart, not a bush, was burning. Desperately, my scientific mind raced as I searched for an explanation. How could it be that God makes defective children? What purpose could it serve?

I found no answer. I had to trust that His ways were higher than my ways. God had a plan for this child who I saw as cheated by God. He looks beyond the disasters of this life to the next life. Perhaps when she died, God gave her a brain of intellectual capacity that would stagger our little minds. I don't know. But I do know that this one night changed my view of life. I understood in my heart that man is made in the image of God.

The Image of God?

Only humans are made in the image of God. What does this mean? Genesis 1:26-27 tells the story of our beginnings—a special creative act by the Triune God. "And God said, 'Let us make man in our image, after our likeness.' . . . So God created man in His own image, in the image of God He created him, male and female He created them."

The image of God is bestowed at the time He creates each new person in the womb at the moment of conception, just as He created Adam and Eve. This image is more than physical development, intellectual capacity, the ability to interact with others, and self-awareness. It is even more than some sort of vague mystical or spiritual part of man separate from his body. It means a moral person accountable to the Creator.

Dr. Paul B. Fowler emphasizes this point in his book, *Abortion, Toward an Evangelical Consensus.*[9] He also states:

> Man does not have a soul, man *is* a soul. Soul in this context does not refer to a distinct aspect of man, but denotes man's body animated by the breath of God. Man does not receive a soul that gets bestowed at some point in development— man is both body and soul. Genesis 2:7 states that "man became a living soul (*being*)."[10]

The human body and soul are intimately united. This is one reason Christ had a resurrected body. It is the reason that we are to receive new bodies—not float around as spirits for eternity. The body-soul fusion is God's masterpiece in man. Contrary to Hugh Ross' interpretation of the soul in Genesis as mere intellect and will, the Bible never states that animals "have a soul" in the New Testament sense. It is unique to male and female humans created in God's image.

Dr. Fowler is a graduate of Wheaton College and Columbia Theological Seminary, with a doctorate from the University of Edinburg. Along with this concept of the image of God, Dr. Fowler emphasizes the importance God places on the moment of *conception.*

Most of us don't care when a baby was conceived—we want to know when it was born! God, however, thinks differently.

Conception is highlighted eleven times in the book of Genesis alone.[11] God wants us to know precisely when He stamped His image on a person. The moment of *conception* is important to God. The example of Jesus in the New Testament repeats this emphasis. Luke 1:31 announces, "And behold, you will *conceive* in your womb and bring forth a son, and shall call His name Jesus." If God considers the act of conception an important event to record in His Holy Scriptures, perhaps we should reconsider our criteria for arbitrarily graduating a person made in His image from potential to full human status.

Understanding the Fetus as Fully Human

Pope John Paul II has beautifully elaborated on the fetus as a person in his 1995 encyclical:

> God proclaims that he is absolute Lord of the life of man, who is formed in his image and in his likeness (c.f. Gen. 1:26-28). Human life is thus given a sacred and inviolable character. . . . From the time the ovum is fertilized, a life is begun which is neither that of the father or the mother; it is rather the life of a new human being with his own growth. It would never be made human if it were not human already . . . this individual person with his characteristic aspects already well determined. Right from fertilization, the adventure of a human life begins, and each of its capacities requires time . . . the results themselves of scientific research on the human embryo provide a valuable indication for discerning by the use of reason a personal presence at the moment of the first appearance of the human life: How could a human individual not be a human person?[12]

The fetus is a unique and interactive person before birth. In Genesis 25:22, Esau and Jacob are described by God as struggling (fighting) with each other inside the womb. This may have seemed beyond belief before ultrasound became available. Now we have even better documentation of unborn babies doing some amazing things. During an operation at Vanderbilt University Medical Center on a twenty-one week old fetus, the baby reached out of the womb and grasped the surgeon's finger.[13]

Dr. Joseph Bruner was kind enough to speak with me personally on 23 February 2000, about fetal operations at the medical center. We discussed these fetal operations to correct spina bifida and the photograph in this book that is referenced in the footnotes. When the initial incision is made into the mother's uterus (womb), the child's hand or foot will sometimes come out. Dr. Bruner told me that this fetal patient in the photograph did grasp his gloved finger when he was touched. This is exactly the same primitive neurological reflex that occurs in a newborn when a parent's finger is grasped tightly by the child.

Ultrasonography has also documented that a fetus can interact on at least some level. During an amniocentesis and other procedures visualized by ultrasound, the fetus can grab for the needle or place fingers over his eyes to shield them from light. The fetal human is indeed a unique, fully human person—fearfully and wonderfully made by God.

Conclusions

The medical facts are clear: Abortion kills a living human being. Physicians have recognized the fetus as a human patient for twenty-four hundred years. God the Father sent Jesus to earth as a fetus. God views conception as an important event to be announced in His Holy Scriptures. God has placed His image upon us at the moment of conception.

Before they met our criteria for graduation from potential status, God interacted with fetal humans on a personal level. Fetal humans can interact and even fight in the womb. Perhaps now you can see why my mind was changed to see the fetus as more than a "potential" person.

In the next chapter, we'll examine the essential role of natural law in the sanctity of God's unique creation—the human person.

Notes

1. Gordon, Hymie, "The Beginning of Human Life," *Studies in Law and Medicine* (Chicago: Americans United for Life, Inc., 1981), as part of the testimony before the Subcommittee on Separation of Powers of the United States Senate Committee on the Judiciary, 1981.

2. Cunningham, F.G. et.al., *Williams Obstetrics,* 20th ed. (Stanford, CT: Appleton and Lange, 1997), 151.

3. *Webster v. Reproductive Health Services,* 492 U.S. 490 (1989).

4. Hippocrates, *Works,* Translator Francis Adams, vol. 1 (New York: Loeb), 299-301.

5. The scientific article may be read in Bruner, et.al., "Fetal Surgery for Myelomeningocele and the Incidence of Shunt-Dependent

Hydrocephalus," *Journal of the American Medical Association* vol. 282, no. 19 (17 November 1999).

6. Peter Singer quoted by Colson, Chuck, and Nancy Pearcey, *How Now Shall We Live?* (Wheaton, IL: Tyndale House Publishers, 1999), 122-123.

7. Thomas, Cal, *Who Cares about Living When the Good Times are Rolling?* (Naples Daily News, 16 July 1998).

8. Brown, Warren S., Murphey, Nancey, and Maloney, H. Newton, *Whatever Happened to the Human Soul?* (Minneapolis: Fortress Press, 1998). These authors seem to have forgotten that the Scriptures speak of mankind as having separate physical and spiritual parts (1 Cor. 5:5).

9. Fowler, Paul B., *Abortion—Toward an Evangelical Consensus* (Portland, OR: Multnomah Press, 1987), 111-114.

10. In many Bible translations, the Hebrew word *nephesh* is unfortunately translated "soul" in Genesis 2:7. *Nephesh* is most frequently translated "person." It is translated this way hundreds of times in the Old Testament. Mankind became a living person or being. The Old Testament use of this word differs from the New Testament concept of a distinct part of mankind. This is one reason why the "soulish animals" argument of theistic evolution may be incorrect.

11. Genesis 4:1, 17, 16:4 (twice), 21:2, 29:33, 30:5, 7, 17, 19, 23, and 38:3-4, 18.

12. Pope John Paul II, *Evangelium Vitae*, 1995 (Origins CNS Documentary Service), 710.

13. Jonathon, a 21-week-old fetal patient at Vanderbilt University Medical Center, is shown grasping the finger of Dr. Joseph Bruner, who is operating with Dr. Noel Tulipan to correct a spina bifida fetal deformity. (See photograph on page 232).

Anaesthesia is utilized on the fetus to perform these operations. The same general anaesthetic that places the mother to sleep will also cause the fetus to become sleepy. Even in this anaesthetized state, just as in adults, sometimes hand and foot motion will occur since the patient is not paralyzed by the medicine. Although Dr. Bruner said that there is controversy over how much pain a fetus can feel, most surgeons are more comfortable with anaesthetizing the fetus due to popular opinion.

The cerebral cortex is not needed to feel pain—only the thalamus, which is functioning at eight weeks. Dr. R. White, Director of Neurosurgery and Brain Research at Case Western Reserve University told a subcommittee in the U.S. House of Representatives, "The fetus within this frame of gestation, twenty weeks and beyond, is fully capable of experiencing pain." An excellent study demonstrated pain response by endorphins in the fetus: M. Fisk, et.al., "Fetal Plasma Cortisol and B-endorphin Response to Intrauterine Needling," *Lancet,* vol. 344 (9 July 1994): 77. See chapter fourteen: Fetal Pain, authored by Wilke, Dr. and Mrs. J.C., *Why Can't We Love Them Both* (Cincinnati, OH: Hayes Publishing, 1997), 94-99.

4.

The Importance of Natural Law

"Who is my neighbor?"

A lawyer asked Jesus that question. Jesus answered with a parable—the Good Samaritan (Luke 10:25-42). The lawyer had hoped for an answer that would ease his conscience. After all, hadn't he just admitted to Jesus that mankind is supposed to love his neighbor as himself? The Lord's answer must have heightened his anxiety. Our neighbor, Jesus explained, is any fellow human in need.

Medical science has determined the fetus to be a living human being. God considers the fetus to be a complete person. Since a fetus *is* a complete living human person who is in need, then a fetus is our neighbor. Christians have believed this since the time of Christ.

Early Church Fathers Speak on Abortion

Barnabas, Clement of Alexandria, Athenagoras, and Tertullian all wrote about protecting the unborn. In *The Epistle of Barnabas* 19.5, we read, "You shall love your neighbor more than your own life. You shall not slay a child by abortion."

In *Paedogus* 2:10.96.1, Clement writes, "Those who use abortifacient medicines to hide their fornication cause not only the outright murder of the fetus, but the whole human race as well."

Athenagorus defended Christians as law-abiding people who are opposed to murder in *A Plea for the Christians* 35.6. "What reason would we have to commit murder when we say that women who induce abortions are murderers and will have to give an account before God?"

Caesarius of Arles wrote, "No woman should take any drug to procure an abortion, because she will be placed before the judgment seat of Christ, whether she has killed an already born child or a conceived one."[1]

In the Didache, a second century catechism for new Christians, we read, "Do not murder a child by abortion or kill a newborn infant." Tertullian, in his *Apology* 9.4, wrote, "It does not matter whether you take away a life that is born, or destroy one that is coming to the birth. In both instances, destruction is murder."

These Christian leaders understood Jesus' command to love our neighbor. To them, the unborn child was a person who qualified as a neighbor. So, they viewed the killing of the unborn child as murder.

What has happened over the centuries to change this view of the unborn human? Do only Christians believe the unborn should be valued as human? Let's search back before the time of Christ.

The Greek and Roman View

Both Plato and Aristotle were philosophical about abortion.[2, 3] Aristotle believed that babies born with deformities should be allowed to die by abandoning the infants to the elements. This is infanticide. In 400 B.C., Aristotle was already warning that a family should have only a few children in order to reduce overpopulation and poverty.

Plato claimed that both abortion and infanticide were legitimate if they were necessary. If a woman over forty years of age became pregnant, she should be *forced* to have an abortion. So what we may have considered modern ideas about this topic are ancient. The common philosophy behind their thinking is that the personal rights of an unborn or deformed person are subservient to the interest of another person or the government.

Since the father was the absolute authority in Roman families, he was able to force the mother to have an abortion. He could even kill his own infant children by abandonment (as advocated by Plato and Aristotle.) This was especially true with newborn females and handicapped children. Unfortunately, this abandonment did not end in ancient times.

Revolutionary Thinking

Jean-Jacques Rousseau, author of *The Social Contract* (1762) agreed. Rousseau argued that the government should free its citizens from the burden of meeting personal obligations. He even proposed that education of the children be taken away from parents to be performed exclusively by the government. His motivation may have had something to do with the several illegitimate children he fathered over the years with his lover, Therese. He abandoned his own children at an orphanage.[4]

But a different kind of revolutionary thinking emerged that was based upon a higher law. The founders of America must have realized the inherent dangers of personal autonomy of choice and abdicating personal responsibility to governmental control. They appealed to the only safeguard against the evils of absolute power from either the government or personal choice. The founders appealed to natural law—the self-evident law of God as the Creator.

Natural law can be found in the *Declaration of Independence*. "We hold these truths to be self-evident, that all men are created equal, that they are endowed by their Creator with certain unalienable Rights, that among these are Life, Liberty, and the pursuit of Happiness."

Natural Law

Although the Bible is not mentioned in the Declaration, and neither is Jesus Christ, natural law recognizes that man was created by God and is therefore responsible to Him. Natural law consists of principles from reason, nature, or nature's God which are ethically binding among humans. Life is the first right of man as made in God's image. Killing another human violates this right. The founding fathers held strongly to this self-evident truth.

The consensus of nations recognized a natural law in the Nuremberg trials. German officers pleaded innocence on the basis that they were only obeying the laws of the government. This Nazi mindset was demonstrated by Rudolph F. Hoess, the German commander at Auschwitz. He . . .

unemotionally described in excruciating detail the operation of his gas chamber. [In his defense he said,] "We were all so trained to obey orders that the thought of disobeying an order would never have occurred to anybody." Hoess was hanged in the Auschwitz compound next to the house where he had lived with his wife and five children.[5]

So, there *is* a natural law that stands superior to national law, international law, and even the autonomous freedom to choose personal happiness. Contrary to current thinking, personal happiness through choice is not the first right in the *Declaration of Independence.* It follows life and then liberty. This was Abraham Lincoln's position when he spoke out against slavery, "No one has the right to choose to do what is wrong."[6]

This priority of natural law is even more important when it comes to the protection of human life. Pope John Paul II spoke supporting this concept of natural law in his 1995, *Evangelium Vitae:*

> Every law made by man can be called a law insofar as it derives from the natural law. But if it is somehow opposed to the natural law, then it is not really a law but rather a corruption of the law. . . . Consequently, a civil law authorizing abortion or euthanasia ceases by that very fact to be a true, morally binding civil law.[7]

This understanding of the supremacy of natural law is critical to the survival of America. George Washington said, "It is impossible to rightly govern the world without God and the Bible."[8] President Harry Truman warned of the consequences of such a departure from our foundation.

> The foundational basis of this nation's law was given to Moses on the Mount. The foundational basis of our Bill of Rights comes from the teachings we get from Exodus and St. Matthew, from Isaiah and St. Paul. I don't think we emphasize that enough these days. If we don't have the proper fundamental moral background, we will finally wind up with a totalitarian government which does not believe in rights for anybody but the state.[9]

Natural law *is* the ultimate authority. It rises higher than governmental law or personal choice. The Christian philosopher, Francis Schaeffer, warned that any other alternative leads to either anarchy or totalitarianism.[10]

Corrie ten Boom and Natural Law

The Hiding Place includes a story that illustrates this principle of natural law. The ten Boom family disobeyed the law to save the lives of Jewish people condemned to die. In this dramatic scene, a mother and her baby find a deliverer:[11]

> And the very next morning into the shop walked the perfect solution. He was a clergyman friend of ours, pastor in a small town outside of Harlem, and his home was set back from the street in a large wooded park.
>
> "Good morning, Pastor," I said, the pieces of the puzzle falling together in my mind. "Can we help you?"
>
> I looked at the watch he had brought in for repair. It required a very hard-to-find spare part. "But for you, Pastor, we will do our very best. And now I have something I want to confess."
>
> The pastor's eyes clouded. "Confess?"
>
> I drew him out of the back door of the shop and up the stairs to the dining room.
>
> "I confess that I too am searching for something." The pastor's face was now wrinkled with a frown. "Would you be willing to take a Jewish mother and her baby into your home? They will almost certainly be arrested otherwise."
>
> Color drained from the man's face. He took a step back from them. "Miss ten Boom! I do hope you're not involved with any of this illegal concealment and undercover business. It's just not safe! Think of your father! And your sister—she's never been too strong!"
>
> On impulse, I told the pastor to wait and ran upstairs. Betsie had put the newcomers in Willem's old room, the farthest from windows on the street. I asked the mother's permission to borrow the infant: the little thing weighed hardly anything in my arms.

Back in the dining room I pulled back the coverlet from the baby's face.

There was a long silence. The man bent forward, his hand in spite of himself reaching for the tiny fist curled around the blanket. For a moment I saw compassion and fear struggle in his face. Then he straightened. "No. Definitely not. We could lose our lives for that Jewish child!"

Unseen by either of us, Father had appeared in the doorway. "Give the child to me, Corrie," he said.

Father held the baby close, his white beard brushing its cheek, looking into the little face with eyes as blue and innocent as the baby's own. At last he looked up at the pastor. "You say we could lose our lives for this child. I would consider that the greatest honor that could come to my family."

The pastor turned sharply on his heels and walked out of the room.

Corrie and her family understood and acted upon natural law—her pastor did not.

Medical Doctors Understood Natural Law

As early as 1859, members of the American Medical Association (AMA) pushed for legislation against abortion because it desired the law to match the medical facts that human life begins at conception. Marvin Olasky quotes the *Transactions of the AMA* in 1859, when he writes:

> . . . major victory came in 1859 when the American Medical Association committee he chaired attacked the "heinous guilt of criminal abortion," recognized the culpability of doctors who were "careless of foetal life," and noted the "grave defects of our laws." The Committee was specific in its recommendation that the AMA declare abortion to be not a misdemeanor but "murderous destruction" . . . passage by the full AMA, however, referred to "unwarrantable destruction of human life," . . . [and] asked that state leg-

islatures "revise" laws concerning abortions and take other
action "as they in their wisdom may deem necessary."[12]

In 1873, legislation was passed to prohibit abortion in
American territories. By the late nineteenth century, all states
had laws protecting the unborn, from conception until birth.
This was because some courageous members of the American
Medical Association had pushed for legislation in 1859. They
desired the law to match the medical facts; human life begins
at conception.

In 1871, the AMA transactions about abortion read, "we
had to deal with human life. . . . No other doctrine appears to
be consonant with reason or physiology but that which admits
the embryo to possess vitality from the very moment of conception."[13] This was written over one hundred years ago. This
truth has been further proven by science—especially ultrasound.
Medical science has saved the lives of premature babies earlier
and earlier in the past fifty years. We are now saving premature
humans at twenty weeks gestation.[14] Unfortunately, we are also
killing them at this age.

Roe v. Wade Denied Natural Law

In 1973, the Supreme Court voted to force legal abortion
on all fifty states up to the ninth month of pregnancy. Justice
Harry Blackmun rejected natural law, scientific evidence, and
legal precedent when he wrote, "We need not resolve the difficult question of when life begins."[15]

Dr. Robert George, Distinguished Chair of Philosophy and
Law at Princeton University, is a signer of the document *We
Hold These Truths*.

> The most egregious instance of such usurpation of power
> is the 1973 decision of the Supreme Court in which it
> claimed to have discovered a "privacy" right to abortion and
> by which it abolished, in what many constitutional schol-
> ars have called an act of raw judicial power, the abortion law
> of all fifty states. Traditionally in our jurisprudence, the law
> reflected the moral traditions by which people govern their
> lives. This decision was a radical departure, arbitrarily
> uprooting those moral traditions as they had been enacted

in law through our representative political process. Our concern is for both the integrity of our constitutional order and for the unborn whom the Court has unjustly excluded from the protection of law.[16]

In 1992, Chief Justice Rehnquist agreed that Roe had no Constitutional basis at all and should be overturned. Although he dissented, the majority of the Supreme Court repeated the tragic error. Notice the unscientific bias of the Court in this quote from *Planned Parenthood v. Casey:*

> Roe's rigid trimester framework is rejected. To promote the state's interest in potential life throughout pregnancy, the State may take measures to ensure that the woman's choice is informed. Measures designed to advance this interest should not be invalidated if their purpose is to persuade the woman to choose childbirth over abortion.[17]

The continued bias of the court majority (five versus four justices) is clearly evident by their use of the term "potential life." Medical science has unanimously defined the unborn human as being alive—not a potential life.

In the previous section, we explored the dangerous precedent this decision made. It gets worse.

> The *Roe's* rule's limitation on state power could not be repudiated without serious inequity to people who, for two decades of economic and social developments, have organized intimate relationships and made choices that define their views of themselves and their places in society, in reliance upon the availability of abortion in the event that contraception should fail. The ability of women to participate equally in the economic and social life of the Nation has been facilitated by their ability to control their reproductive lives. The Constitution serves human values, and while the effect of reliance upon *Roe* cannot be exactly measured, neither can the certain costs of overruling *Roe* for people who have ordered their thinking and living around that case be dismissed.[18]

Did we read the words of the Supreme Court correctly? "Serious inequity to people?" Is it unreasonable to expect people to be "burdened" with the inconvenience of having to change their way of thinking and behavior in order to save the lives of millions of humans?

Planned Parenthood—the pro-abortion rights group—emphasizes that, "The ability of women to participate has been facilitated by Roe." What happened to the participation of over seven hundred thousand females who are killed in the womb each year? What about the ability of *those* females to participate in the economic and social life? Isn't *that* a serious inequity?

If we use the Court's *same line of reasoning*, why did we ever allow the slaves to go free? Why should slave owners have been inconvenienced to change the way that they had become accustomed to doing business for a century? It certainly affected *their* ability to "participate equally in the economic and social life of the Nation!" The slave owners certainly "made choices that define their views of themselves and their places in society, in reliance upon the availability of " slaves.

Intelligent people—even Supreme Court justices—can be irrational. The Supreme Court of 1857 made the same mistake with slavery. Thank God that Abraham Lincoln had the courage to stand up for what was right. Our present Supreme Court majority continues to evade the critical right to life of the living human being in the womb. Inaccurate and misleading terms such as "potential life" become poor attempts to hide the atrocity that every abortion kills a *human*.

The Dred Scott Decision Denied Natural Law

The Supreme Court used the same semantic game to deny natural law rights to black Americans. The Dred Scott decision was based upon politics—governmental law to appease popular opinion.

Although African-American people were recognized as humans, blacks were not "persons." This allowed blacks to be acknowledged as humans but treated as less than human. The result was the continued abuses of slavery, including death. There was no penalty for murdering a living black human "nonperson."

The economic and political advantages to abuse "nonpersons" were too great to pass up. As a result, the economic and political and human losses of the Civil War were too great to imagine.

In October 1999, I listened to Dr. Robert George articulate the importance of natural law at the Wilberforce Conference. Chuck Colson writes about him in the book, *How Now Shall We Live?*

> Robert George of Princeton University has pressed these arguments among the nation's leading scholars, including well-known deconstructionist Stanley Fish of Duke University. In 1998, George was invited to debate Fish at a meeting of the American Political Science Association: The debate would be about the nature of the evidence for and against abortion. In earlier writings, Fish had dismissed arguments against abortion as based on "religious conviction" alone, while suggesting that the case for abortion is based on "scientific facts." George's position held that, on the contrary, the arguments against abortion are based on scientific data that a fetus is indeed human.

> George sent his paper to Fish in advance, and then the two joined two hundred other scholars who had gathered for the debate. But the event was cut short at the start when Fish rose, threw his own paper on the table, and announced, "Professor George is right, and he is right to correct me. Today, the scientific evidence favors the pro-life position."

> The audience sat in stunned silence.[19]

Conclusions

The early Church fathers viewed abortion as murder. It violated natural law and Jesus' command to love our neighbor as ourselves. This was contrasted with the Greek and Roman views that were not based upon natural law. Even children after birth could be killed at will.

The atrocities of the German Holocaust and the Civil War were due to a denial of natural law. President Truman warned that we must return to our moral foundation if America is to survive. The other challengers for absolute power—autonomous freedom of choice and governmental law—inevitably lead either to either anarchy or totalitarianism.

With this sobering understanding, we explore the next critical question in this journey. Is the killing of an unborn human murder?

Notes

1. Fowler, P., *Abortion—Towards an Evangelical Consensus*, 17. The origin is unknown.

2. Aristotle, *Historia Animalium* 7.3 and *Politics* 7.1.1, 7.14.10.

3. Plato, *Republic* 5.9, translated by Robin Waterfield, *Republic* (Oxford: Oxford University Press, 1993), 175.

4. Rousseau, Jean-Jacques, *Confessions*, vol. 1 (New York: Dutton, 1904), 314-316.

5. Cronkite at Nuremberg, accessed 3 February 2000; available from http://www.geocities.com/Athens/1942/world_court.html.

6. Abraham Lincoln, Lincoln-Douglas Debates, from two separate quotes. The sixth-13 October 1858, ". . . but if you admit that it is wrong, he cannot logically say that anybody has a right to do wrong." The seventh-15 October 1858, "But if it is a wrong, he cannot say people have a right to do wrong." Accessed 11 February 2000; available from http://www.umsl.edu/~virtualstl/dred_scott_case/texts/deb7.htm, pages 6 and 17.

7. Pope John Paul II, *Evangelium Vitae 1995* (Origins CNS Documentary), 715.

8. Federer, William J., *America's God and Country-Encyclopedia of Quotations* (Coppel, TX: Fame Publishing Inc., 1994), 660.

9. Ibid., 589.

10. Schaeffer, Francis, *The Complete Works of Francis A. Schaeffer: A Christian Worldview*, vol. 5, A Christian View of the West (Wheaton, IL: Crossway Books, 1982), 150, 430, 483-491.

11. ten Boom, Corrie, *The Hiding Place* (Minneapolis: World Wide Publications, 1971), 112-113.

12. Olasky, M., *Abortion Rites: A Social History of Abortion in America* (Wheaton, IL: Crossway Books, 1992), 117-118. He quoted the

Report on Criminal Abortion, submitted by American Medical Association Committee on Criminal Abortion at the Twelfth Annual Meeting in Louisville, Kentucky, May 1859, *Transactions of the AMA,* 1859.

13. Report of the Committee on Criminal Abortion, *Transactions of the American Medical Association,* 1871. Confirmed by Robert J. Tenuta, AMA Reference Archivist, 28 February 2000.

14. *The Miami Herald* carried the story of baby Kenya King's first birthday. She was born at twenty-one weeks and weighed eighteen ounces (6/9/86, article #8602140008). Even seven years ago, the survival rate was 79 percent at twenty-five weeks at the Johns Hopkins in Baltimore as reported by Allen, M., et.al., "The Limit of Viability," *N. Eng. J. Med.,* vol. 329, no. 22, (25 November 1993): 1597.

15. *Roe v. Wade,* 410 U.S. 113 (1973).

16. George, R., et. al., *We Hold These Truths,* accessed 23 July 1999; available from http://www.welchfoundation.org.

17. *Planned Parenthood v. Casey,* 505 U.S. 833 (1992).

18. Ibid., 855-856.

19. Colson, C., and Nancy Pearcey, *How Now Shall We Live?,* 131.

Murder or Merely Killing?

If someone kills a fetus, is it murder?

I'd like to avoid asking that question for the sake of those who've experienced pain from their decision to have an abortion. However, it must be asked. The purpose of this chapter is not to make my friends and other women feel guilty. It is to show the truth.

As Jesus said, when truth is embraced, it does not condemn us—it sets us free. The women who have succeeded in their struggle against guilt have been those who have acknowledged God's truth. Why? Because that truth does not end with guilt and condemnation—it leads us on to the liberty of God's genuine and *complete* forgiveness.

Criminal Abortion

I still have my medical dictionary from 1977, when I entered medical school. The other day I looked up the word *abortionist* in the 1974 edition. I read, "one who makes a business of inducing criminal abortions."[1] The definition is the same in a 1932 pocket edition with only one exception—the word *criminal* is not used in the earlier dictionary. Because of medical doctors, the business of abortion began to expand in the 1960s.

Physicians were at the forefront to help protect unborn children one hundred years ago. But, as in Hitler's Germany, when doctors violated the Hippocratic Oath (natural law), the nation followed. Our nation liberalized abortion laws during the 1960s to include cases of rape and incest, and for various health reasons. The Model Penal Code in 1962 was the impetus for these changes which opened the door for *Roe v. Wade*. New York was the first state to introduce abortion on demand.

The modification of New York's Penal Law 125.00 made it legal for a licensed physician to perform an abortion in the first twenty-four weeks of gestation. Abortion was still a homicide after twenty-four weeks.[2] Alaska, Hawaii, and Washington then followed with similar changes which legalized the killing of the unborn human at earlier stages in his or her growth.

The Roe and Bolton Decrees

In 1973, the Supreme Court stripped away states' rights to regulate abortion in any way during the first trimester of pregnancy. In addition, abortion could be performed through the ninth month if the mother's "health" was affected in any manner. That included emotional health for an inconvenient time to have a child.

Abortion became a fundamental right. Suddenly, the word "person" in the Fourteenth Amendment did not apply to the unborn. In 1998, over 95 percent of abortions were performed for the convenience of the dead child's mother.[3]

Today, abortion is still legal in all fifty states through the ninth month of pregnancy. A woman can legally abort her child the very day before her due date.

President Ronald Reagan mourned this atrocity in 1984 in a book, *Abortion and the Conscience of the Nation*: "Our nationwide policy of abortion-on-demand through all nine months of pregnancy was neither voted on by our people or enacted by our legislators."[4]

The U.S. Supreme Court of 1973 declared that "legal personhood does not exist prenatally."[5] This distortion of words directly contradicted precedents and subsequent decisions.

More Recent Court Decisions

In 1989, in *Webster v. Reproductive Health Services*, 492 U.S. (1989), a more honest U.S. Supreme Court allowed a Missouri statute to stand which stated that human life begins at conception. It also stated that the *Roe* decision based upon a viability timeline should be discarded. Instead, the 1989 decision established that the Court has a "compelling" interest in fetal life throughout pregnancy.[6]

Today, Ohio, Missouri, Minnesota, and Pennsylvania all have laws that treat the unborn child as a legal human being. The unborn have a legal right to inheritance. In Ohio's *Ebb v Smith* of 1979, a will from a deceased person requested equal distribution of money to all relatives "living at the time of my death." The Ohio court ruled that this included a fetus in the womb at the time of the relative's death.[7]

Massachusetts, Oklahoma, South Carolina, and Pennsylvania have had state legislative or Supreme Court decisions establishing punishments for murder of a fetus as a person. About half the states now have some sort of feticide law. In 1998, twelve states had laws that grant the fetal human victim status in a crime throughout the nine months of pregnancy. Another fifteen states grant victim status to the unborn child during the later stages of growth in the womb. Twenty-seven states have passed bans on one type of late abortion—partial-birth abortions.[8]

Sadly, sixteen states continue to operate under the "born alive" rule. With this legal fossil, the injured child must survive for a brief period after birth before a crime has been committed. If a 9-month-old, fullterm baby is being delivered in natural childbirth but is killed prior to exiting the birth canal, no crime has been committed.

A Case of Legal Murder

In 1997, in the state of Indiana, Melanie Elmore was shot in the abdomen during a drive-by shooting. Both she and her husband survived. However, her 8½-month-old fetus was killed by shotgun pellets. The two brothers, Troy and Judge Hatchet, were charged with feticide. The two could not be charged with murder, however, because an unborn child is not legally considered a person until birth in Indiana.

Representative James Buck introduced a bill to give legal standing to the fetus because of this injustice. Although the bill was passed by the legislature, Governor Frank O'Bannon vetoed it saying that he feared it would make doctors who perform abortions criminally liable. Fortunately, the legislature could see through this excuse and voted to override his veto—the House by a margin of eighty-seven to nine and the Senates by thirty-seven to twelve.[9]

The Governor's excuse for his veto highlights our schizophrenic American thinking. Reasoned thought tells us that the fetus is a living human worthy of protection. But, we continue to believe that the mother can legally choose to kill her unwanted child at eight and a half months—the same age as Elaine's unborn child. I was born six weeks premature. According to this thinking, I was not a "person." My mother could have aborted me. (Thank you, Mom.)

Our medical advances have made it possible to save babies born as early as twenty weeks. Yet we continue to allow abortions at the same age. Does it really matter whether the doctor, mother, or someone else kills the child? The child is dead.

A Key State Statute

Pennsylvania amended the state Title 18 in 1997. The law was changed in order to acknowledge the rights of the unborn person in natural law; it imposed penalties on the degree of murder—just as in adults.

The first penalty category, aggravated assault on an unborn child, is a first-degree felony. The second category is murder in the first, second, or third degree. First-degree murder of the unborn carries a sentence of death or life in prison. (The penalty for second-degree murder is life imprisonment and not more than forty years for third-degree murder.) The actual law reads:

> THE SENTENCE FOR A PERSON WHO HAS BEEN CONVICTED OF FIRST DEGREE MURDER OF AN UNBORN CHILD SHALL BE THE SAME AS THE SENTENCE FOR MURDER OF THE FIRST DEGREE EXCEPT THAT THE DEATH PENALTY SHALL NOT BE IMPOSED.[10]

California has also ruled that the killing of a fetus is murder.

California Law on Fetal Murder

The Supreme Court of California stated it this way in 1994: "California law defines murder as the 'unlawful killing of a human being, or a fetus, with malice aforethought.' . . . We conclude that viability is not an element of fetal homicide under section 187, subdivision (a)."[11]

A charge of murder could be brought against a defendant after the fetus was seven weeks gestational age in the uterus. Why did the Court see a need to change the law to punish the murder of a fetus?

The state of California changed the penal code after a husband purposely killed his 35-week-old baby in the womb of his wife. In *Keeler v. Superior Court,* the husband rammed his knees in to his wife's abdomen when she was thirty-five weeks pregnant. He told his wife, "I'm going to stomp it out of you." Doctors performed an emergency C-section but the child was stillborn—it had died with a fractured skull. Keeler was charged with murder under Section 187 which used the common law definition: "Murder is the unlawful killing of a human being, with malice aforethought."[12]

The man was acquitted because the child, by California law, was not a human being until after it was born alive. Enraged, the state passed the feticide law—recognizing the fetal human as a legal person.

Now, California and Minnesota, both require life imprisonment as the penalty for murder of a fetus. In Massachusetts, the viable fetus was specifically given the status of "human being" in *Commonwealth v. Lawrence*, 404 Mass. 378, 536 N.E. 2d 571 (1989).

Born Alive Rule is Obsolete

An Oklahoma court gave a woman an eight-year prison term for the manslaughter of a fetus in a drunken driving accident in 1994.

> Advances in medical and scientific knowledge and technology have abolished the need for the born alive rule. Specifically, the medical and scientific evidence before us establishes that the child within Poole's womb was a living, viable fetus at the time of the collision and that the child died as a result of the placental rupture which occurred when Poole's stomach hit and broke the steering wheel of her car. . . . In conclusion, we reject the born alive rule and hold that a viable human fetus is a "human being" against

whom a homicide as defined in Section 691 may be committed.[13, 14]

The Oklahoma decision quotes the Supreme Court of Massachusetts in 1984, which stated:

> In keeping with approved usage, and giving terms their ordinary meaning, the word "person" is synonymous with the term "human being." An offspring of human parents cannot reasonably be considered to be other than a human being, and therefore a person, first within, and then in normal course outside, the womb.[15]

Uncommon "Common Sense"

My 13-year-old daughter, Rachael, was able to see through Justice Blackmun's statement that the living, growing fetus "represents only the potentiality of life."[16] In her essay on abortion as murder in 1999, she agreed with many state Supreme Court justices. "If a fetus isn't a human life, then what is it? It's alive, so . . . it must be some new life form!"[17]

Fortunately, many state penal codes are catching up to the advances in science and beginning to reverse some of the absurd conclusions and effects of the *Roe v. Wade* decision.

Arkansas Law on Fetal Murder

Arkansas is one of the twenty-six states in which prosecutors are able to bring criminal charges in the death of an unborn child. On 26 August 1999, Shawana Pace was pregnant and almost due to deliver her child when she, her son, and her boyfriend entered their house one night. A burglary was in progress.

One of the intruders told Shawana, "Your baby is dying tonight." In the attack, she suffered injuries that included a ruptured spleen—an operation was required to remove it. Her baby, weighing almost seven pounds, died.

Shawana suspected that her boyfriend was involved since he did not want the child. The police questioned the teenage suspects—Derrick Witherspoon, Lonnie Buelah, and Eric Buelah. They were all brothers and were friends of Shawana's boyfriend.

The three suspects told police that the boyfriend had hired them to stage a robbery at his own house in order to kill the baby. Bullock and the three youths were charged with capital murder, which carries a sentence of life in prison or the death penalty.[18]

The Law Turned Inside Out

What's the difference between a *legal* abortion and the *illegal* murder of an unborn child? The only difference is whether or not the mother wants the child. Let's look at a hypothetical example.

Suppose two women in Portland, Oregon, become pregnant on the same day. Six months later, one woman delivers a premature baby girl. The physicians and nurses do everything possible to save the life of the child for the couple who was previously childless. Fortunately, their child does well with expert care in the intensive care unit.

The second mother decides that she cannot afford the inconvenience that this child inside her will create. She walks into an abortion clinic. The physicians and nurses work diligently to perform a partial birth abortion. The child's body is completely out of the mother's womb–all except for the child's head. The child is killed with a thrust of the scissors to the brain. The brains are sucked out of the head and the skull collapses.

As the child's limp body is being thrown into the garbage, the first child is abducted from its crib in the hospital. The kidnapper drives across the Columbia River to the state of Washington, but the baby girl dies due to the lack of needed medical attention.

The woman who abducted the child could be charged with murder. The woman who aborted her child cannot. What's the only difference between the two cases? Both fetuses were the same age. Both fetuses were outside the mothers' bodies. Both could have survived.

One was legally killed because the child was *not* wanted by her mother. The other child was illegally killed because she *was* wanted by her mother. From the perspective of the unborn children, there is no difference between abortion and murder— either way, both children are dead.

This blatant inconsistency of law may also be demonstrated in our present court system dealing with fetal drugs and alcohol. In 1992, Cornelia Whitner was sentenced to eight years in prison for addicting her unborn child to crack cocaine.[19] She could have avoided prison by legally killing him by abortion before birth.

Deborah Zimmerman was tried in Wisconsin on attempted first-degree intentional homicide when witnesses testified that she had been intoxicating herself in order to "kill this thing" in her womb. The Wisconsin Supreme Court divided three to three on the verdict.[20]

God Views Abortion as Murder

In Exodus 21: 20-25, we read God's law about a pregnant mother who is hurt by men fighting. As a result, her child is born prematurely. A few of the modern paraphrases, including *The Living Bible* and *The New American Standard Bible,* use the word "miscarriage" for the Hebrew word *yatsa.* Miscarriage implies the death of the child. The Hebrew word literally means "to go out" and is never used in the Bible to refer to a miscarriage. The correct translation is "premature birth."[21]

A child may "go out" prematurely—be born prematurely—but no injury occurs. In this case, the husband and judges determine the penalty on the man causing the accident. A local newspaper carried an article in 1999 about a woman eight months pregnant who was in a car accident. The baby was born prematurely as a result of the accident, but the baby lived and was not injured.[22]

However, injury may occur to the child. Moses states that the man who injured the child must receive the same injury as the child's. If the injury causes death, the man must pay with his life, ". . . if injury follows, then you will give life for life, eye for eye, tooth for tooth" (Exod.21:23).

The conclusion is evident from the punishment—to kill an unborn or premature child is a grave sin.[23]

Old Testament scholar, Professor Bruce K. Waltke saw this passage differently. In a 1967 symposium, he claimed that according to Exodus 21:22, the fetus is not a person with value equal to the mother. Since then, he has done an about-face.

Delivering his presidential address at the twenty-seventh annual meeting of the Evangelical Theological Society in 1975, Waltke admitted that his former position was "less than conclusive for both exegetical and logical reasons," and his conclusion now was that the fetus is indeed a human being; abortion is murder.[24]

I cheered for this good man and was reminded of Dostoevsky's question in *The Brothers Karamazov*. "Is it really so wonderful in these days to find a man who can repent of his [error] and publicly confess his wrongdoing?"[25]

But, my heart also ached for him. What would it feel like to know that a bad decision may have contributed to the deaths of millions of humans? Was it the pressure of the pro-choice movement of the time? Did Christians around him believe that the fetus was subhuman? Was it a desire to protect the "really important Scripture" and not have the church caught up in the politics of the debate? Perhaps, one day, I will get to ask those questions of him.

Conclusions

American law was based upon the truth that killing an unborn human is murder. Current legal precedents punish criminals who murder the unborn. The logic and common sense of natural law require it. Killing an unborn child is murder. What does God want us to do about it?

Notes

1. Dorland's Illustrated Medical Dictionary (Philadelphia: W.B. Saunders, 1974), 4.

2. *State Abortion Laws,* accessed 23 July 1999, available at http://members.aol.com/_ht_a/abtrbng/abortl.htm.

3. U.S. Department of Health and Human Services, Center for Disease Control, 1997.

4. Reagan, R., Koop, C.E., *Abortion and the Conscience of the Nation* (Nashville, TN: Thomas Nelson Publishers, 1984), 15.

5. *Roe v. Wade,* 410 U.S. (1973).

6. *Webster v. Reproductive Health Services,* 492 U.S. (1989).

7. "Legal Status of the Unborn," Ohio Right to Life, accessed 11 July 1999; available from http://www.ohiolife.org/lex/fetallaw.htm. *Ebb v. Smith,* Ohio Supreme Court (1979) resulted in Ohio Revised Code §2109.34, and §2307.131. All of these now provide financial legal rights to the unborn.

8. *National Right to Life News* (January 2000): 13; and *Feticide Laws,* accessed 23 July 1999; available from http://members.aol.com/_ht_a/abtrbng/feticide.htm.

9. "Indiana State Senate Overrides Governor's Veto of Feticide Law," *The Pro-life Infonet,* accessed 10 February 2000; available from http://www.euthansia.com/indiana.html.

10. General Assembly of the Commonwealth of Pennsylvania, Title 18, Sections 102(C), 106(A)(1) and (B)(1), 108 and 1102, Amended–1997 Session. Accessed 11 July 1999; available from www.peopleforlife.org/s45.html. See also *The Philadelphia Inquirer* of 9 April 1999 where the Superior Court of Pennsylvania ruled the unborn a "person."

11. *People v. Davis,* California Supreme Court, 872 p.2d 591 (1994).

12. *Keeler v. Superior Court of Amador County,* 87 Cal Rptr., 481, 470 p.2d, 617 (1970).

13. *Hughes v. The State of Oklahoma,* 868 p.2d 730 (1994).

14. The defendant did not have to serve her sentence because the court ruled that it had not previously made clear that a fetal homicide was equivalent to the murder of a human.

15. *Commonwealth v. Cass,* 392 Mass. 799, 467 N.E. p.2d 1324 (1984).

16. *Roe v. Wade,* 410 U.S. (1973).

17. Wilson, R., Oregon Right to Life Essay Contest, 1999, Second Place.

18. "Arkansas Charges Four in Feticide Death," *Pro-life Infonet,* accessed 7 September 1999, #2008 from erfelt@prolifeinfo.org.

19. *Whitner V. State of South Carolina,* No. 2446 (1997). She pled guilty to criminal child neglect, S.C. Code Ann. §20-7-50 (1985), accessed 24 July 1999; available from http://aol.com/_ht_a/abtrng/whitner.htm.

20. "Wisconsin Supreme Court Split on Alcohol Abuse to Unborn Children," *Geocities*, accessed 11 July 1999; available from http://www.geocities.com/CapitolHill/2054/alcoholabuse.html.

21. Sproul, R.C., *Abortion—A Rational Look at an Emotional Issue* (Colorado Springs, CO: Navpress, 1990), 198.

22. Sivesind, Cam, "Pregnant Canby woman hurt in accident, passenger in car dies," *The Canby Herald* (16 June 1999): 1.

23. Although some people attempt to say that the pregnant woman is the one receiving the injury, this does not fit with the context. Punishments for murder and injury in men and women are already prescribed earlier. The woman is given equal value to the man. This is seen in the command to put to death a child who physically abuses a father or mother or curses a father or mother (Exod. 21:15, 17). The woman's equal value is again seen in Exodus 21:20 where a man who hits a maid with a rod will be put to death if she dies. Therefore, the emphasis in 21:22 is not the woman, it is the *pregnant* woman—a woman with a living person—a child—inside her. The Hebrews had no separate word for the unborn such as our term "fetus." It was a *child* to them—a living person. One word, "*yeled,*" was used for the unborn fetus and the born infant.

24. Fowler, P.B., *Abortion—Toward an Evangelical Consensus*, 74.

25. Dostoevsky, D., *The Brothers Karamazov* (Norwalk, CT: The Easton Press, 1979), 228.

God's Priority of Life

There is not another living thing in the universe that is made in the image of God—only mankind. According to His Word, protecting His pinnacle of creation is top priority. So to God, murdering one individual of His special species is a most grave sin.

Each of us may have our own view of what constitutes a serious sin or crime. In Papua, New Guinea, anger is considered a worse sin than murder. Treachery is valued as the highest virtue. In fact, when Christian missionaries first told the natives the story of Jesus, the natives *cheered* when Judas betrayed Jesus.

Here in America, most people agree that murder is one of the most serious sins. Does that mean that sin is relative? Does it *change* from society to society? Sin may be relative among societies, but not to God. An understanding of God's view of sin as recorded in the Bible will help us.

The First Societal Law

After destroying the world by a flood for its wickedness and violence, God gave his first societal law with a prescribed punishment. It preceded even the Ten Commandments. God gave it to Noah and his family. "Whoever sheds man's blood, by man shall his blood be shed; for in the image of God made He man" (Gen. 9:6).

This foundational law was designed to prevent the violence that was prevalent prior to the flood. Murder was to be punished by the execution of the murderer. The reason, according to God, was that people have a high intrinsic value. The murderer forfeits his very life as punishment. His execution tells the world that a valuable innocent person was murdered.

God knew what our society has discovered in the past few years. People who commit serious crimes are at high risk for repeating crimes. In fact, 63 percent of criminals released from U.S prisons are rearrested for a felony or serious misdemeanor within three years; and 47 percent of state inmates were in prison for a violent offense.[1] Preventing such criminals from ever returning to society would immediately drop our felony crime rate! Only by God's grace can such people be rehabilitated to honor God's first law.

God's Image Is Only For Humans

The fact that man alone has been created in the image of God, divides Christianity from the environmentalists who demand equal protection of animals and insects.

The *Oregonian* newspaper in January 2000, carried a story about two boys who dragged a dog behind a car and then stabbed it to death. The title of the article was "Dog Killer gets maximum sentence:" It read, "Descutes County Juvenile Court referee Stephen P. Forte told Joseph R. 'Rocky' Henderson of La Pine that his actions in the early morning hours of November 28, were comparable to the dragging death of an African American man in Texas last year."[2]

Think about this fact. The death of a dog is being compared to the death of a man—a black man made in the image of God. The dog is an animal—a lower creature. God has given man a mandate to care for this earth and the animals. The juvenile *should* be punished for his act. But, to compare the death of a black man (who was made in God's image) to the death of a dog is not a comparison God sees.

It gets worse. According to the article,

> The incident sparked an avalanche of letters, e-mails and calls to Forte, the district attorney's office and the local newspaper. Forte noted in court that many of the letters demanded that the boys be treated in the same fashion in which they had treated the dog(s).[3]

Should the boys be tied to a car, dragged, and then stabbed to death like the dog? The Bible says, "*No.*" God gave mankind the birds and animals as food to eat (Gen. 9:3). People in some cultures still eat dogs for meat to survive. God recognizes a vast difference in value between men and animals.

Since we humans were given the responsibility to care for God's creation, we should be concerned about other living things.[4] However, other parts of creation are not equal in value to mankind.

The absurdity of the example above is one reason why Chuck Colson has pressed so hard for a biblical worldview. Even the Christian conscience has deteriorated to the point that we become more upset about one animal dying than millions of humans being murdered by abortion. God help us.

Murder Is Not Loving

According to Jesus, the proof of loving God with all of our heart and soul and mind and strength is to love our neighbor as ourselves. That means that we recognize and respect him or her as being created in the image of God; and, as being valuable to Him, irrespective of *our* opinion of the individual.

To murder my neighbor is to violate God's priority commandment between persons in society. To murder my neighbor is the ultimate antithesis of "loving my neighbor as myself."

Murder: The Gravest Sin between Persons

For many millennia, murder has been accepted as the most serious crime or sin throughout the world. This is evidenced by the punishments for murder compared to punishments for other crimes. This pattern can be traced back to the law given to Noah after the flood.

Other sins or crimes directly against God may be more serious. For example, unbelief is eternally fatal. But in "horizontal" relationships of person to person, there is no greater sin than murder.

Classic literature also reflects this concept. Dante, in the Inferno section of *The Divine Comedy*, places Judas and Brutus in the worst part of Hell. Their treachery resulting in murder was punished the most severely.

Abortion *does kill* an innocent human being made in God's image. Therefore, abortion is also murder. Abortion murder is one of the most serious crimes which can be committed between persons in society.

The widely respected evangelist, Billy Graham, agrees with this conclusion. "We can demonstrate God's love, but we must never think that we can solve one moral crisis by condoning another, especially the crime of murder, for unrestrained abortion is nothing less than that."[5]

Pope John Paul II has clearly pronounced the killing of an unborn child to be the serious sin of murder:

> The moral gravity of procured abortion is apparent in all its truth if we recognize that we are dealing with murder and, in particular, when we consider the specific elements involved. The one being eliminated is a human being at the very beginning of life. No one more absolutely innocent could be imagined.[6]

Murder by Degrees

Our American legal concept of first, second, and third degree murder comes from the Jewish Torah. God placed "Thou shalt not kill" in the Ten Commandments. In Hebrew, the word "kill" is *ratsach*, and means "murder." God gave Moses a detailed law to punish persons who committed murder.

If a man planned to kill another man and waited to kill him, this was first degree murder and carried the most severe punishment (Lev. 24:17). However, if the killing was *not* premeditated, the punishment was less severe (Num. 35:22). If the killing was unintentional or accidental, the killer was sentenced to live the remainder of his life within a confined city until the high priest died (Num. 11:25). These laws were prescribed to protect God's priority of human life.

Authorizing Murder Is Still Murder

We don't have to commit a murder personally to be responsible for one. Authorizing or asking someone else to murder another human also makes us responsible. This was highlighted in the Nuremberg trials after World War II. The world watched in complete disbelief as the German officers on trial defended their killing of innocent humans. Nazi officers made many attempts during the Nuremberg trials to defend the murders as only following orders. "The prisoners were not *humans*; and, the killings were *legally* authorized."[7]

These officers did not personally kill anyone. Yet each one was convicted of murder because they authorized murder. The court decided that the murder of an innocent human was so serious that an officer should have known not to authorize such an order.

Authorized murder has been most publicized in organized crime circles where "bosses" order the murder of certain individuals. The most infamous crime boss convicted in the recent past is John A. Gotti. The head of the Gambino crime family in New York, he was earning about ten million dollars a year. He authorized the murder of the top crime boss in a coup to be number one. *The Clenched Fist*, by Marilyn Bardsley, describes the scene immediately following the murder:

> Terrified pedestrians scattered every which way, while the shooters escaped along their prearranged routes. In moments, another Lincoln carrying two men passed by Sparks to survey the results of the carefully executed plan. John Gotti and his colleague Sammy the Bull Gravano and the conspiratorial group of ten men called the Fist had pulled off the first major gangland assassination since Albert Anastasia had been hit in 1957. In the next few days all New Yorkers and much of the rest of the world would know the name John Gotti as he skyrocketed to fame as the daring new head of the Gambino crime family.[8]

It took seven years to bring John Gotti to justice for authorizing the murder, but justice was finally served. Why? American law views authorizing a murder as equivalent to murder.

Unintentional Murder

In August 1998, in the State of Arizona, Marvin Evans was convicted of criminally negligent homicide. Mr. Evans, a 69-year-old man driving his vehicle with a suspended license, ran a stop sign and killed Salvador Silva, who was driving another car. The elderly man showed remorse for the death. He did not *intentionally* kill another human being. He did not *directly* kill the man—the car accident killed him. Mr. Evans was still sentenced to prison for murder. When a human dies from the negligence of someone else, we recognize the responsibility of the negligent party.

Here's what the New York Penal Law states:

> Criminal negligence means that a person engages in conduct which creates a substantial and unjustifiable risk that another person's death will occur, and when he or she fails to perceive that risk, and when the risk is of such a nature and degree that failure to perceive it constitutes a gross deviation from the standard of care that a reasonable person would observe in this situation.[9]

If the defendant perceived the risk and proceeded anyway it would be first or second degree murder.

Criminal negligence is established if the defendant acts intentionally, knowingly, or recklessly. *Intentionally* means that the person desired to engage in the act or cause the result. *Knowingly* means that the person is aware that his or her conduct is reasonably certain to cause the result of death. *Recklessly* means that the person is aware of the risk but chooses to disregard it (the substantial and unjustifiable risk that the act will produce the result.) Any of these three conditions will result in a guilty verdict.

Unintentionally Authorizing Murder

Exodus 21:28-29 provides a foundational basis for this natural law:

> If an ox gores a man or a woman that they die, then the ox will be certainly stoned and his meat will not be eaten. But, the owner of the ox will be clear. But, if the ox had a history of pushing with its horns and the owner had been notified, and the owner did not keep the ox penned, but it killed a man or woman, the ox will be stoned and his owner will also be put to death.

Why is the owner punished so severely? Because the owner knew the risk of death to another human from his choice not to act, yet decided to keep the ox alive for his own benefit. The owner did not intentionally or personally kill anyone, so the death was unintentional, accidental, and indirect.

God views a person as culpable for murder if that person has a higher priority than protecting a human life, when known

to be at risk of death. When neglect *indirectly* and unintention-
ally causes the death of someone, God calls it murder.

This is a serious statement about choices. The fetus is our
neighbor—a human person at risk for death. If we choose other
priorities in voting, we allow the fetal human to be killed. Does
God hold me responsible for this neglect?

God does think differently than we do. In Isaiah 55:8, God
says, "for my thoughts are not your thoughts and my ways are
not your ways." The passage commands us to seek out the Lord
while He may still be found (so that He may be gracious) as we
view God's standard for justice and culpability.

When Naboth refused to sell his vineyard to Israel's king,
Ahab stormed off like a spoiled child, "laid down on his bed
and turned away his face and would not eat any food."[10]

Ahab's wife, Queen Jezebel, took over. " 'Aren't you the
government of the kingdom of Israel? Rise up, eat food, and let
your heart be merry. I will give you the vineyard of Naboth, the
Jezreelite.' So she wrote letters in Ahab's name and sealed them
with his seal" (Isa. 55:7).

The queen commanded the leaders of the city to hire false
witnesses to accuse Naboth, then put him to death. Those
leaders obeyed, and Naboth was indirectly killed. Yet God holds
King Ahab directly responsible for this murder of Naboth even
though the King never touched the man, or requested any action to be taken. Here's how God's prophet, Elijah, accuses
King Ahab: "Thus saith the Lord, Have you killed and also
taken possession? And thus shall thou speak to him saying,
Thus saith the Lord, In the place where the dogs licked the
blood of Naboth, shall the dogs lick thy blood, even thine" (Isa.
55:19).

King Ahab later died in battle under unusual circumstances.
Although he didn't intentionally authorize a death, his
covetousness—the desire to have something more for himself—
resulted in the murder of Naboth.

Christians who choose other priorities at the cost of innocent human life plod in the footsteps of sin for which God
killed King Ahab. We may prefer not to believe that our thoughts
and actions result in murder. God seems to think differently.
God declared King Ahab guilty. How will we, who vote for a
pro-choice candidate, escape?

Conclusions

God destroyed the world with a flood because of man's violence—especially murder. His priority following the flood was to prevent the murder of innocent people made in His image. Today, with the murders of millions of innocent babies each year, American society may surpass even the wickedness of the pre-flood world.

One of our highest priorities should be to stop the mass murders of abortion. God judges those who choose other priorities. Since God's priority is life, shouldn't we—His Church—be modeling this to others?

Notes

1. *Criminal Offenders Statistics,* U.S. Department of Justice, Bureau of Justice Statistics, accessed 10 February 2000; available from http://www.ojp.usdoj.gov/bjs/crimoff.htm.

2. Gregory, G., "Dog killer gets maximum sentence," *The Oregonian,* 11 January 2000, B1.

3. Ibid., B5.

4. The Christian should be concerned about the environment—but as a less important priority. Campolo, T., *How to Rescue the Earth Without Worshipping Nature* (Nashville: Thomas Nelson Publishers, 1992).

5. Graham, B., *Storm Warning,* 236.

6. Pope John Paul II, *Evangelium Vitae 1995,* 710.

7. Cronkite, W., *Cronkite at Nuremberg,* accessed 3 February 2000; available from http://www.geocities.com/Athens/1942/world_court.html.

8. Bardsley, M., *The Clenched Fist* (Dark Horse Multimedia, Inc.), accessed 9 August 1999; available from http://www.crime-library.com/john/johnmain.htm.

9. New York Penal Law; Penal Law 125. 10, class E Felony, accessed 23 July 1999; available from http://ucs.ljx.com/cji/art12510.htm.

10. I Kings 21:4.

The Church Modeling
God's Priority

Children learn more about what we truly believe from what we *do* than what we *say*. I had never heard my father make a statement about the value of human life. But one afternoon, when I was twelve, I saw with my own eyes what he believed.

My father is a meticulous man. We children used to complain to each other that room checks were done military style, even though no white glove was used. Everything was to be organized and spotless.

On the afternoon in question, a young woman collapsed in the street in front of our house. Dad picked her up and carried her inside our home while mom called the ambulance. With concern for the woman on his face, he carried her into my bedroom and carefully laid her bloody, unconscious body on my clean bed. As the blood dripped onto my spotless sheets, I learned more about the priority of human life than many hours of talks could have conveyed.

What Are We Modeling?

As God's Church, we are to teach His priority. What we do has far more impact than what we say. It's commendable for Church leaders to proclaim that abortion and euthanasia are wrong. (Some even call it sin.) But what do we teach by our behavior?

Once in a church meeting the entire service was centered on the persecuted Church around the world. The pastor did an excellent job of recounting the atrocities in Sudan, China, Indonesia, Egypt, etc. He then asked for people to pray, give money, and contact congressional leaders–to influence those politicians to stop the persecution of Christians (and other religious groups) around the world.

Since thousands of believers were dying each year for their faith, his strong stand was commendable. Still, my heart was heavy as I left the church building that morning. Six months earlier, the same pastor had said it *was political* to tell Christians how to act on the millions of humans dying each year from abortion right here in America.

The discrepancy became even more apparent many months later. I returned to that same church when many were observing Sanctity of Life Day, since the church had a reputation for participating in prior years; but, the only acknowledgment by the leadership this day was a ninety-second prayer by the youth pastor. In the sermon, the pastor proclaimed that God was able to help the church raise money to fund the building program, so that they could minister to more people. This may have been needed, but couldn't it have waited one more week?

How could good leaders, who love God, not see their own inconsistency? Sadly, when it comes to the abortion murder of humans, even church leaders can be deceived. What is the conclusion of the people from these omissions? God's priority of human life is not really that important.

Getting Serious

The Church must be educated in word and in deed. Randy Alcorn, author of the popular book *Deadline*, addresses that fact in *Pro-Life Answers to Pro-Choice Arguments*:

> Church leaders must take responsibility for the sad state of the church just described. . . . The desire to be popular and avoid people's disapproval is a common reason for church leaders to hold back in pro-life efforts. But for every reason we have we must be ready to answer a question on the last day: "Was that reason more important than the lives of all those children?"

> Martin Luther addressed the pastor's role in facing the greatest evil of his day:

> If I profess with the loudest voice and clearest exposition
> every portion of the truth of God except precisely that
> point which the world and the devil are at that moment
> attacking, I am not confessing Christ. Where the battle
> rages, there the loyalty of the soldier is proven, and to be
> steady on all the battlefronts besides is mere flight and
> disgrace if he flinches at that point.[1]

The Enemy has attacked the value of human life in America
through abortion, infanticide, euthanasia, senseless killings, and
suicides. Yet the Church—for the most part—has not yet realized
the seriousness of this threat to our God-given right to life.

The Problem

A voter opinion poll conducted in Oregon in 1999 requested opinions on abortion. Voters were asked, "Do you consider yourself pro-choice or pro-life on the question of abortion?"[2]

These are the percentages of pro-choice Christians: Mainstream Protestants were 52 percent pro-choice, Catholics 39
percent, and Evangelicals 23 percent. These are Christian voters who "fly the flag" of pro-choice. This does not even count
the many Christians who say they are pro-life yet vote consistently for pro-choice candidates! The only time they ever vote
pro-life is on a ballot measure.

In doing so, they continue to contribute to the deaths of
millions of babies whom God loves. Why? The leadership of
the Church has not taken a stand, and then modeled it. George
Barna agrees:

> Christians today do not live in a way that is quantifiably
> different from their non-Christian peers, in spite of the
> fact that they profess to believe in a set of principles that
> should clearly set them apart. We tend to rely upon a
> cultural filter rather than a biblical filter for interpreting
> events, information, experiences, and opportunities. . . .
> Most Christians have plentiful exposure to God's truth
> and exhortations but few have actually been pierced by the
> truth, principles, and meaning of the Christian faith.
> Christians do not behave differently because they do not

think differently, and they do not think differently because
we have never trained them, equipped them, or held them
accountable to do so.[3]

Leaders aren't modeling! No wonder Randy Alcorn chastised the leadership for failing in their responsibilities. Most
leaders seem unwilling to "carefront"—confront in love. How
are Christians ever going to know God's priority if the leadership does not take a stand for the truth? Luther's question is
right on target—are we merely professing or are we actually
confessing Christ?

The Responsibility of Leadership

There is no tougher job in the world than being a pastor
or church leader—not even a parent. For, usually, a parent has
the opportunity to train a child from birth. A pastor must take
over the training after all of the bad attitudes and habits are
already in place!

Most churches continue to have unreasonable expectations
of pastors' responsibilities. Even so, year after year, these servants continue to extend God's grace. But the burnout rate is
high.

God makes it plain that we are to obey those in authority
over us (Heb. 13: 17). These same leaders are going to have to
give an account of how they carried out their responsibilities.
They are to teach us the truth and be sure that we obey it. We,
however, are not to make their work a burden by disobedience—
or *we* will be held accountable.

Some qualifications for leadership are explained in Titus
1:9: "holding fast the faithful word as he has been taught, that
he may be able by sound doctrine both to exhort and to confute
the opposers."

However, in almost all cases, the church pays the pastors'
salaries; that makes it dangerous for them to speak the truth.
After all, people don't like being told that they are sinning and
will receive God's judgment if they don't repent. That kind of
faithfulness to God's Word could cost a pastor his job. Never-
theless, it is the job of God's servants to speak the truth.

Many ministers have placed themselves in the position of
politician rather than *proclaimer* of God's truth. In the 30 Oc-

tober 1999 issue of *World* magazine, Marvin Olasky hits the
nail squarely on the head:

> Those who convert to Christianity should also convert to
> a style of thinking opposed to the self-worship that under-
> lies many aspects of pro-choice thought. Successful poli-
> ticians build coalitions within a pro-choice culture, but
> ministers must be willing to offend. It is folly to tell
> political leaders that they must be bold and courageous
> when so many leaders within the church are not: Much of
> what comes from major pulpits is soft, man-pleasing
> rhetoric more worthy of a politician than a preacher. For
> that reason, many who accept Christ as savior have no idea
> what it means to take Him as Lord, and they never fully
> move away from self-worship.[4]

Ministers of the gospel have an obligation not only to teach
God's truth, but to do it in an uncompromising manner. Sin
must be called the sin that it is. People must be commanded
(and expected) to repent and do right. While discharging this
responsibility has never been a winner in the politics of the
Church, it will definitely be a winner in the Kingdom of God.

Spines of Steel or Straw?

My pastor, whom I love, once told me that he desired to
have Christians in the Church with "spiritual spines of steel."
I like that analogy because that is exactly what we'll need if we
are to endure a future persecution. How can we possibly lay
down our lives as martyrs, boldly proclaiming that Jesus is the
Christ, if we don't even have the courage to speak God's truth
to those within the Church who might be offended? Are our
spiritual spines made more of straw than steel?

To some, the idea of persecution in America may seem
unlikely. Others are aware that mild persecution is already taking place through loss of jobs and freedom of speech.

I doubted until the fall of 1999, when I was sitting in a
doctor's lounge waiting to perform an operation. The tragic
crash of EgyptAir flight 990 was being investigated. Another
surgeon, whom I knew to be a moral man, was watching television in hopes of finding out the cause. He spoke in a con-

cerned tone: "It was probably one of those Christian Fundamentalists who did it."

When moral, intelligent people have been so brainwashed by the media as to draw these conclusions, we may be closer to Nero's Rome than we think! How can Christians withstand such persecution when we are too afraid to stand up for our unborn neighbor, when it is easy now?

Modeling Leadership

Dr. Paul Fowler points to academia's failure to stand with spines of steel on abortion.

> Many Christian colleges and bible schools hold no official position on the abortion issue. Yet, often the faculty of these schools must sign a pledge every year vowing not to smoke or drink—minor issues in comparison.[5]

This timidity among leadership is not new, as Dietrich Bonhoeffer reminds us:

> If the Church refuses to face the stern reality of sin, it will gain no credence when it talks of forgiveness. Such a Church sins against its sacred trust and walks unworthily of the gospel. It is an unholy Church, squandering the precious treasure of the Lord's forgiveness. Nor is it enough simply to deplore in general terms that the sinfulness of man infects even his good works. It is necessary to point out concrete sins, and to punish and condemn them.[6]

He also warns us that those who take a stand for God's holy priorities will suffer.

"The messengers of Jesus will be hated to the end of time. They will be blamed for all divisions which rend cities and homes. Jesus and his disciples will be condemned on all sides for undermining family life, and for leading the nation astray; they will be called crazy fanatics and disturbers of the peace."[7]

Jesus Himself was accused of being used by the Devil to destroy God's work in Israel. In fact, the religious leaders of the day accused Him of having a demon. Some of us have been accused of being used by Satan to sidetrack the vision and work of the local church.

Yes, the Enemy is at work. The question is, who is being influenced? Is it those who stand with God's priority of life? Is it us who steer the Church in a wrong direction? Or, is Satan again blinding the eyes of religious leaders?

R.C. Sproul observes that people love the prophets of God—but only if they are dead.

> In Jesus' day the Old Testament prophets were venerated. They were the great folk heroes of the past. Yet, when they were alive they were hated, scorned, rejected, persecuted, and killed by their contemporaries. People have an appreciation for moral excellence, as long as it is removed a safe distance from them. The Jews honored the prophets from a distance. The world honors Christ, from a distance. Peter wanted to be with Jesus, until He got too close. Then Peter cried, "Please leave."[8]

Modeling Life as the Priority

Rather than resist God's prophets, it may be beneficial to hear them seriously. God calls the Church to embrace moral excellence—especially by standing up for the sanctity of life. If we keep praying for revival without acting on God's priority, I fear that God has already given His answer.

> I hate, I despise your feast days, and I will not take delight in your solemn assemblies ... Take away from me the noise of your songs, for I will not hear the melody of your harps. But let justice run down like waters, and righteousness like a mighty stream. (Amos 5:21-24)

Saint Ignacious, Bishop of Antioch in 106 A.D., chastised the church at Smyrna for failing to model the love of Christ—by caring for the poor, widows, orphans, and the afflicted. Pope John Paul II wrote:

> At such a time, Christians must act. This is a fundamental demand not only of discipleship but also of democracy, which flourishes when "people of conviction struggle vigorously to advance their beliefs by every ethical and legal means at their disposal" (*Living the Gospel of Life*, 24). ... Your action needs to be both educational and political.[9]

Perhaps God will send revival when we model *His* priority of justice and righteousness—especially in working to save tiny innocent lives who have been unjustly condemned to death.

Conclusions

Church leaders are called to teach God's priority. Jesus described that as seeking first His kingdom in all areas of life. This includes voting. A high percentage of Christians continue to sin because they vote pro-choice. To obey God, the Church must teach that voting for a pro-choice (to kill humans) candidate is a serious sin.

Leaders must model a change in priorities to love our unborn neighbor by saving his or her life. We must model that priority so others will see. That requires spines of steel. I'm disappointed in the time that I've personally wasted—pursuing lesser priorities—and have repented. God will hold me accountable. Now my aim is to teach other Christians to save the lives of helpless ones by their words and by their actions.

I've changed my priorities. Will you do the same? If you will, let's ask the next question: Does God really expect us to bring the voting booth inside the church?

Notes

1. Alcorn, R., *Pro-Life Answers to Pro-Choice Arguments* (Portland, OR: Multnomah Books, 1994), 223.

2. Moore, B., *Impact of Abortion Views on Voting Decisions,* Moore Information, Public Opinion Research (21-22 January 1999).

3. Barna, G., *The Second Coming of the Church* (Nashville: Word Publishing, 1998), 121-122.

4. Olasky, M., "A pro-choice culture," *World* (30 October 1999), 34.

5. Fowler, P., *Abortion—Toward an Evangelical Consensus,* 14.

6. Bonhoeffer, D., *The Cost of Discipleship* (New York: MacMillan Publishing Co., 1976), 324.

7. Ibid., 239.

8. Sproul, R.C., *The Holiness of God* (Wheaton, IL: Tyndale House Publishers, 1995), 58-59.

9. Pope John Paul II, Homily at Central Park, 7 October 1995.

Is Voting Only a Political Issue?

What can we do to stop the mass killing of babies? The answer may seem obvious: use our power in the voting booth. But a voice in the back of our heads may object. *A Christian should stay out of politics.*

A Princeton poll in 1996 revealed that one out of every three Christians did not even bother to vote in the presidential elections.[1] This neglect may have been due to fatigue or faulty theology. Whatever the reason, the result is the same—we are failing to meet our obligations as Christians. The Lordship of Jesus Christ should extend to every aspect of our lives.

St. Paul explains this in his letter to the Colossians: "And whatever you do in word or deed, do all in the name of the Lord Jesus Christ, giving thanks to God the Father through Him" (Col. 3:17).

He commands slaves to work diligently for their masters like they were working for God Himself—in the fear of God. He then repeats the command:

> And *whatever you do*, do it heartily, as unto the Lord and not to men, knowing that from the lord you will receive the reward of the inheritance; for you serve the Lord Christ. But he who does wrong will be repaid for what he has done, and there is no partiality. (Col. 3:23-24; emphasis mine)

Where I come from, "whatever you do" means *whatever you do*. That command includes a slave working sincerely for his master in fear of God. That also includes voting. God sees no dichotomy between the secular and the spiritual.

Pastor D. James Kennedy reminds us of a great Dutch Christian in his book, *What if The Bible Had Never Been Written?*

Do Christianity and the Church have something to say about politics, or is politics completely outside the purview of the Church? Some people think that the Bible and Christianity address only spiritual issues.

Abraham Kuyper, the greatest theologian Holland ever produced, was both an influential Christian and a politician. Not only was he a tremendous scholar, founder of the Free University of Amsterdam, an exegete of the Scriptures, and a minister of the gospel of Jesus Christ, but his talents were so outstanding that he became the prime minister of Holland. He was so effective a prime minister that the government declared a national holiday to celebrate his seventieth birthday. . . . Kuyper wrote:

"The Son is not to be excluded from anything. You cannot point to any natural realm or star or even descend into the depth of the earth, but it is related to Christ, not in some unimportant tangential way, but directly. There is no force in nature, no laws that control those forces that do not have their origin in that eternal Word. For this reason, it is totally false to restrict Christ to spiritual affairs and to assert that there is no point of contact between him and the natural sciences."[2]

The Politics of Religion

Now some Christians will immediately respond that "the Church is not to be involved in politics." What's the truth about the Church and politics?

Unfortunately, most Americans believe that Thomas Jefferson would have supported our presently imposed separation of church and state. When he wrote this phrase in a letter to the Danbury Baptist Association in 1802, he was referring to the concept of a state religion—not the free exercise of religion in American society. While President, Thomas Jefferson attended worship services held in the Capitol building, sent an abridged Bible to the American Indians, and later started a church that met in the Charlottesville, Virginia courthouse.[3]

Our present misunderstanding of separation of church and state was conjured up by Supreme Court decisions beginning in 1947 in the case of *Everson v. Board of Education,* and most egregiously in 1971 with the "Lemon Test" of *Lemon v. Kurtzman*.[4] This lemon would not have passed the founders' test. Thomas Jefferson, (or any other founding father), would have been shocked by the current deconstructionist history that rejects the strong influence of a personal Creator, God, in our government. Actual quotations from the founders of this nation demonstrate that they voiced a separation of the state from an official religion, not the complete separation of religion from government and public society.[5]

In 1954, the United States government began prohibiting churches from "political speech." It seems that a tax-exempt foundation granted money to an opponent of then-Senator Lyndon B. Johnson. So, he supported a law to prevent tax-exempt entities from giving financial support to political candidates.[6] The tax-exempt status of our churches has been chained to our conformity to this law.

As a result, today, most pastors would not consider preaching boldly and specifically on what the Bible says about political or social issues. Most pastors are not aware that the law only prohibits speaking for or against a *specific* candidate. There is no prohibition to keep the pastor from fulfilling his holy duty—instructing the Church on how to apply God's biblical standards of sin and holiness when voting. The result is a Church without moral guidance about sin when voting. Voting is a spiritual issue.

Logical Fallacy

Let's take a little closer look at that often repeated statement: "The Church is not a political body." Of course, that's true. But a logical evaluation—*reductio ad absurdum*—will expose the fallacy of this thinking through the following syllogism:

Major premise: The church is not a political body.
Minor premise: Voting is political.
Conclusion: The Church should not be involved in voting issues.

Therefore, it is also true that:

Major premise: The Church is not a bank or financial institution.

Minor premise: Banks and financial institutions collect
money and distribute it.
Conclusion: The Church should not collect money and
distribute it.

And,

Major premise: The Church is not a symphony orchestra.
Minor premise: A symphony orchestra plays music that
evokes emotions.
Conclusion: The Church should not play music that evokes
emotions.

The error in logic becomes apparent. There is no compelling reason for the Church to avoid the topic of voting. There
is, in fact, a compelling spiritual reason for the Church to
become involved in voting—the lives of our unborn neighbors
are at stake! Do we love our neighbors enough to try to save
them? Or, are we afraid of men?

The Almighty Tax Exempt Status

Loss of tax-exempt status hangs over the head of the Church
in America like an anvil dangling over a frightened mouse.
Sometimes we seem to protect it more carefully than God's
own truth.

The Church at Pierce Creek has come face to face with this
dilemma as reported in *Christianity Today*.[7] Rev. Little asks,
"Has tax exemption become a means for government to control
the church? Evidently, the government thinks so. And by their
meticulous compliance, many pastors, church boards, and Christian leaders seem to support that position."[8]

In his response to the IRS summons for records, Reverend
Little also asks the right questions:

Are we being examined because politics has recently crossed
the moral boundaries, which have been so clearly defined
in the Holy Scriptures for four millennia?

Are you saying that, Because the abandonment of these
biblically established moral laws is now established, as
political policy, that these moral issues have now been
lifted out of the church's domain?

> . . . if at any time moral issues become carefully couched in
> the language of political policy that the IRS is set to say that
> the tax exempt church no longer has a right to address those
> issues. Isn't that giving over to the State what actually
> belongs to the church? And what happens if all moral law
> becomes political? (Ibid.)

This is a critical question. We can be certain that the government will not stop with abortion. Why? Because it has already moved on to homosexuality. State and local laws are
already being passed to give homosexual partners the same legal
rights as a married man and woman. The most recent state
Supreme Court to follow this God-forsaking pattern is Ver-
mont, on 20 December 1999. The public does not know the
standards in God's Word. Why should the government stop? It
knows that the pulpits of America can be controlled. The voting gag is in place.

Church History

The American government already has an excellent model
for isolating the Church into spiritual irrelevance. The German
government under Hitler used the same tactics and they worked.
Consider this quote from Nazi officer, Josef Goebbels, in 1935:

> To educate the young people into religious ways may
> perhaps be the task of the Church, but to educate the young
> in politics is very much our affair. . . . The youth belong to
> us and we will yield them to no one. . . . For the Churches
> there is only one solution, which will ensure peace: Back
> into the sacristy. Let the Churches serve God; we serve the
> People.[9]

Or, perhaps a word from Adolf Hitler on 24 October 1933:
"We have brought the priests out of the Party political conflict,
and led them back into the Church. And now, it is our desire
that they should never return to that area for which they were
not intended."[10]

The government was serious about keeping the Church
from impacting society in practical ways. How did the Church
respond? Much the same as the churches in America have responded today.

[The] Nazi State pursued a completely single-minded policy to drive the Churches out of political life. Many evangelical pastors argued that the Nazi Party's drastic limitations of Church activities were to be regarded, not as a defeat, but rather as a liberation from a dangerous overextension of ecclesiastical influence into the political arena.[11]

We, the Church, must not lose sight of our primary objective—a spiritual *and* physical kingdom where Christ will reign. But the retreat of the Church from the daily matters of society ended with disaster. This retreat was partly to blame for the millions of deaths in the Holocaust.

In *The Nazi Persecution of the Churches, 1933-1945*, we learn the seeds of Lyndon B. Johnson's misguided prohibition of 1954 and the Church's response.

Many of them (the clergy) were so deeply shocked by the tumultuous course of events in the first year of the Nazi rule that their only wish was to withdraw from political involvement of any sort. Both their sense of loyalty to established power and their theological leanings, strongly influenced by the Pietistic tradition, inclined them towards a purely "spiritual" ministry, concerned only with individualistic salvation and ethics, and a readiness to obey the government's orders under all circumstances. On the account they were prepared to accept the Nazi dictum that "politics do not belong in the Church."[12]

What will happen if the churches in America continue to allow the government to dictate the place of the Church in society? We have already witnessed it in Germany. Dietrich Bonhoeffer and Corrie ten Boom stood up to this government as unlawful—a violation of natural law and God's law. They did this because they understood the parable of the Good Samaritan.

Love Thy Neighbor as Thyself

When we take a closer look at the parable, we realize that Jesus was calling his followers to action. When a lawyer asks, "Who is my neighbor?" Jesus unfolds the story.

A man traveling from Jerusalem to Jericho was robbed, beaten, and left half dead on the side of the road. One religious man and then another passed by on that same road. They both saw the dying man in need. Both of them moved to the other side of the road to avoid helping the dying man. They had other priorities.

A Samaritan passed by and saw the man's desperate plight. He demonstrated compassion by treating the wounds and then bandaging them. Clearly, he changed his priorities to place the man on his own donkey and take the dying man to a place of recovery. Not only that, but he paid for the man's physical needs for food, clothing, and shelter out of his own money. The Samaritan then agreed to pay whatever it cost for the man to recover—to allow him to live.

Now for the "clincher." Jesus asks, "Which of these three men was a neighbor to the man in need?" The lawyer answers correctly, saying, "The one who showed mercy on him." Jesus said, "Go and do the same."

The moral is clear: It's sin to go around on the other side of the road without helping that dying person to live.

Loving as the Priority

Jesus' words include persons in the womb. Unless we show them that kind of compassion, the unborn will be victims of fatal abortion violence. But, if we have mercy on the dying and act to save their lives, we will have loved our neighbor.

To love our dying neighbor, we must change our priorities. Instead of ignoring him, Jesus asks us to act and save him from death.

Many of us are like the religious leaders of Jesus' day. In our case, we walk by on the other side of the road crying "politics" to drown out the pleas of the dying.

Voting for Love as the Priority

The religious leaders didn't hurt the dying man on the road. They didn't contribute to his injuries in any way. Perhaps, they even prayed for the man's healing, or for his eternal soul. Still, they sinned because they did not act in love to save their neighbor.

Christians know that millions of humans will die from abortion; however, they have other priorities than saving the lives of those at risk, when it comes to voting. Christians who vote for pro-choice (to allow killing of humans) candidates do *not* vote to stop the murder of those babies. In the parable of the Good Samaritan, Jesus indicates that *those* Christians are guilty. Those Christians who choose to vote for another priority are guilty of contributing to abortion murder.

Now, it's not that they injure the babies, or that they want the babies to be injured. As a matter of fact, these Christians may have voted for other very good causes. But they did not change priorities to rescue those dying human neighbors. God holds people responsible for acts of omission or commission when that action results in the *death* of a human.

Voting Pro-choice Is a Sin

We shouldn't be surprised that voting can be sinful. God's Word warns that even a spiritual exercise like prayer can be sin. King David understood this when he asked God in Psalm 109:7, "When he shall be judged, let him be condemned. Let his days be few, and let his prayer become sin."

In Luke 18:9-14, Jesus tells of a Pharisee whose prayer was founded on a trust in his own righteousness instead of a need for God's forgiveness. The socially hated tax collector was declared righteous by God, while the prestigious Pharisee's sin of pride caused even his spiritual prayer to be sin.

Proverbs 28:9 also proves this point. "He that turns away his ear from hearing the law, even his prayer is an abomination." Yes, even prayer can be a sin. Since even prayer can be a sin, shouldn't we give careful consideration to the question of whether voting could also be a sin?

Here is what Pope John Paul II says on the subject: "In the case of an intrinsically unjust law, such as a law permitting abortion or euthanasia, it is therefore never licit to obey it, or to "take part in a propaganda campaign in favor of such a law or vote for it."[13]

Let's remember that God's view of sin is different than ours. He implicates not only those who commit the act, but all those who did not act to stop the murders and help the victims. This is covered in the *Evangelium Vitae*:

As well as the mother, there are other people too who decide upon the death of the child in the womb. In the first place, the father of the child may be to blame, not only when he directly pressures the woman to have an abortion, but also when he indirectly encourages such a decision on her part by leaving her alone to face the problems of pregnancy. . . . Doctors and nurses are also responsible. . . . But responsibility likewise falls on the legislators who have promoted and approved abortion laws . . . on the administrators of the health care centers where abortions are performed.[14]

We must change our thinking to conform to God's standard of sin. If we do not, we will be unpleasantly surprised when we stand before Him.

Dr. Robert George, Professor of Law and Philosophy at Princeton University, explains why we fail to love our neighbor when we vote for another priority rather than saving human life:

One who wills that someone have the choice as to whether to destroy an unborn child necessarily wills that the child be denied the legal protections against direct killing that one wills for oneself and others whom one considers worthy of the equal protection of the laws. Someone who supports legislation or public policies that exclude the unborn from these basic protections *violates the Golden Rule.* Someone who acts on a proposal to deprive the unborn of legal protection against abortion unavoidably renders himself complicit in the injustice of abortions that his actions help to make possible. Someone who by free choice renders himself complicit in the evil of abortion corrupts his own character thus *placing his soul in dire jeopardy.*[15] (emphasis added)

Voting can indeed be a serious spiritual matter.

Chuck Colson[16] and George Barna[17] agree that Christians must become involved in our society—socially and politically. Pastor D. James Kennedy, author of *Evangelism Explosion*, has heralded a similar call for the Church to awaken:

Let us not repeat the lesson of the German church in the 1930s and 40s that stood apathetically by and watched as the unwanted of their generation were marched off to unspeakable death. We need Corrie ten Booms . . . who will stand up to man's repudiation of God's law and follow Jesus' command to love our neighbor as ourselves.[18]

The Reformed theologian, R.C. Sproul, issues a strong warning:

It is clear that abortion is considered by many to be only a moral issue. This has led to the prevalent opinion that opposition to abortion involves an unwarranted intrusion of the church into the public domain. . . . Though Christians and churches may at times overstep the boundaries and improperly intrude their religious concerns, I do not think that this is the case with abortion. There is no greater arena of common grace and common concern than human life. . . . The struggle against abortion is difficult, but it is worthy.[19]

Pope John Paul II speaks clearly on this political involvement of the Church: "If charity is to be realistic and effective, it demands that the Gospel of life be implemented also by means of certain forms of social activity and commitment in the political field as a way of defending and promoting the value of life."[20]

A common theme emerges in the writings of all these Christian leaders—the biblical principle of "love of our neighbor." Not to vote, or to vote for the wrong priority, is sin.

Conclusions

Voting on abortion is not a political issue—it is a spiritual issue. There is a proven history of danger to society if the Church continues to avoid the public sphere. The risk of non-involvement outweighs the risk of involvement. This is true both for society and for our own personal judgment before God.

We must act on voting as a spiritual issue—before it is too late. That voting includes saving the lives of unborn persons. If we love our neighbors in the womb, we must change our priorities to rescue them from death. It is a sin to elevate other priorities above God's priority of voting against abortion killing. Does this mean we have no concern for women? In the next chapter, we will look at some interesting facts.

Notes

1. Parmelee, L., *The Roper Center,* 24 February 2000, Job #23-RS-056. The Princeton Survey Research Associates performed this survey on 1/14/98 through 1/18/98. Protestants and Catholics were equally negligent by not voting—30 and 34 percent respectively. In fact, all of the demographics for age, race, party affiliation, etc. were somewhat comparable except for one—only 37 percent of people age eighteen to twenty-nine voted. The older the American (even over 80-years-old), the more likely they were to vote. People with incomes less than ten thousand dollars per year were also less likely to vote.

2. Kennedy, D.J., *What if the Bible Had Never Been Written?* (Nashville: Thomas Nelson Publishers, 1998), 60.

3. Beliles, M.A., *Thomas Jefferson's Abridgement of the Words of Jesus Christ of Nazareth* (Charlottesville, VA: Providence Foundation, 1993), 3-24.

4. Simon, B.A., Esq., "The roots of church/state separation," Freedom Writer, November/December 1996, accessed 24 February; available from http://www.berkshire.net/~ifas/fw/9611/roots.html. No update noted.

5. To read quotations from these men about their personal God, who they believed to be active in shaping America, I suggest Federer, W.J., *America's God and Country: Encyclopedia of Quotations* (Coppell, TX: Fame Publishing Co., 1994).

6. *Churches, Free Speech, and the Regulations of the IRS Regarding Elections,* The American Center for Law and Justice, accessed 10 February 2000; available from http://www.aclj.org/irs501.html, 10-11.

7. *Christianity Today* (14 December 1992): 146.

8. Terry, R., *Why Does A Nice Guy Like Me . . . Keep Getting Thrown In Jail?* (Lafayette, LA: Huntington House Publishers, 1993), 150.

9. Conway, J.S., *The Nazi Persecution of the Churches 1933-45* (New York: Basic Books, 1968), 114-115.

10. Moeller, H., *Katholische Kirche und Nationalsozialismus* (Munich 1963), quoted by Conway, J., *The Nazi Persecution of the Churches, 1933-45*, 65.

11. Conway, J.S., *The Nazi Persecution of the Churches 1933-45*, 134.

12. Ibid., 78.

13. Pope John Paul II, *Evangelium Vitae 1995*, 715.

14. Ibid.

15. George, Robert, *Conscience and the Public Person* (Dallas, TX: 10th Annual Bishops Conference, 1991), 217-233.

16. Colson, C., and Nancy Pearcy, *How Now Shall We Live?*, 414-417.

17. Barna, G., *The Second Coming of the Church*, 207.

18. Kennedy, D.J., Foreword to Randall Terry, *Operation Rescue* (Huntington House Publishers, 1993).

19. Sproul, R.C., *Abortion—A Rational Look at an Emotional Issue*, 156.

20. Pope John Paul II, *Evangelium Vitae 1995*, 720.

Pro-Choice: Does It
Help or Hurt Women?

The Christian friend I mentioned in the beginning of this book, is also a supporter of women's rights. This is one of the reasons she has difficulty voting for pro-life candidates. According to the media, feminists must champion the reproductive rights of women. The idea is, "Feminists always vote pro-choice." But this hasn't been the historical position of those who stood for women's rights, and it's not the position of many feminists today.

Women's Rights

The name, Susan B. Anthony, stirs the souls of feminists, and rightly so. This brave woman pioneered women's suffrage. Willing to be thrown in jail for what she believed, Anthony illegally cast a ballot in the presidential election in 1872. Sure enough, she was arrested and jailed. Modern feminists' support of her fight for voting rights helped produce the Susan B. Anthony one dollar coin in 1979.

With that in mind, the essay Anthony wrote and published in *The Revolution*, about the "horrible crime of child murder," is shocking to some today.

> Guilty? Yes, no matter what the motive, love of ease, or a desire to save from suffering the unborn innocent, the woman is awfully guilty who commits the deed. It will burden her conscience in life, it will burden her soul in death; but, oh! Thrice guilty is he who, for selfish gratification, heedless of her prayers, indifferent to her fate, drove her to the desperation which impels her to the crime.[1]

Feminists for Life, an organization of women who understand the critical link between respect for fetal life and the rights of women, stand with Anthony. "Women will never climb to equality and social empowerment over mounds of dead fetuses," according to Sidney Callahan—feminist, author, and psychologist.[2]

Fates Chained Together

This may sound like a morbid statement, but the author understands a key principle. The oppressor is chained to the person whom she oppresses—their fate is joined.

Booker T. Washington, writing in 1895, said it first:

> There is no escape through law of man or God from the inevitable:
>
> The laws of changeless justice bind
>
> Oppressor with oppressed;
>
> And close as sin and suffering joined
>
> We march to fate abreast.[3]

America continues to suffer as a result of our shameful treatment of black Americans—both before and after the Civil War. The laws may have changed, but sinful attitudes toward our black brothers and sisters continue. It is not enough to avoid hurting them or not to be prejudiced. We must be proactive to encourage and support them.

In October 1997, I was in Washington, D.C., for a Promise Keepers event. During a break, thousands of men took to the same water fountain, the one where I was standing in line. After a long wait, a black man struggled to fill his water container. He held it with one hand and pushed the button with the other, but the lid on his container kept flipping down. After I pressed past several men and began pushing the button for him, a flash from a camera took me by surprise. Why would anybody take a picture of this?

This wasn't an event that would make the headlines—only one white helping a black man get a drink of water. But, we don't need huge acts of service to heal America. We do need to stand together. Our fates are joined together—that includes pro-life issues. Feminists for Life understand this principle.

Fetus Lovers versus Women Lovers

The pro-choice movement has often used the media to portray pro-life persons as "fetus lovers," saying, "They have no concern for the woman." To keep abortion legal and widely available throughout the nine months of pregnancy is *truly* caring for the mother, they claim. Is this true? Let's look at some facts.

Pro-life clinics across the nation help women who choose *not* to murder their babies. They provide money, clothes, housing, and even help in finding adoptive families. Emotional counseling is available for women with Post-abortion Syndrome. These services are provided without cost.

In contrast, abortion is a money-making business. Abortion clinics do not perform abortions for patients who cannot pay. The mother's welfare is *not* the primary concern. In fact, women are lied to about the risks of abortion and what is being aborted.

Pro-life people do love fetuses, and why not? They are fully human persons made in the image of God. Pro-life people also love women. They love them enough to tell them the truth.

Risks Include Death

The abortion murder industry has a unique place in the medical community. Why? Because it doesn't have to follow the same rules of other medical procedures.

There is no requirement to inform or educate the mother through simple and painless ultrasound pictures that the tissue inside her is moving, looks like a human, and has a beating heart at eight weeks. Fortunately, in some states such as Texas, new laws have mandated the disclosure of this information to the mother.

Complications *do* occur in abortions. Some of these include massive abdominal infection, perforation of the uterus leading to death, severe blood loss that can result in death, parts of the fetal body being left in the womb, etc. The list of possible complications is fairly long. The *OB-GYN Observer* reported that "87 percent of 486 obstetricians and gynecologists had to *hospitalize* at least one patient this year due to complications of legal abortion."[4]

> Complications following abortions performed in free-standing clinics is one of the most frequent gynecologic emergencies . . . encountered. Even life-endangering complications rarely come to the attention of the physician who performed the abortion unless the incident entails litigation. The statistics presented by Cates represent substantial under-reporting and disregard women's reluctance to return to a clinic, where, in their mind, they received inadequate treatment.[5]

Double Standards

Doctors have been prosecuted in the United States for *killing the mother* while trying to perform an abortion.[6] Allegations were, in part, that no emergency treatment was given. In most states, abortion chamber clinics are *not* required by law to have emergency equipment available.

Even veterinary clinics are required by law to have emergency equipment available for the animals. Yet, the Supreme Court claims that we do not "want women to be unduly burdened with rules against abortion."[7]

Outpatient Surgical Centers must be certified by the Joint Commission on Accreditation of Healthcare Organizations in order to receive Medicare payments and most insurance payments. When operations are performed on patients, there are specific guidelines to ensure the safety of those patients. Abortion murder facilities have no such rules. They are exempt from the rules that even *tattoo parlors and hair salons* must obey!

Abortionists do not see their patients again. Follow-up is *expected* in a doctor-patient relationship. This lack of it is unconscionable for an operative procedure with a risk of death.

There is no peer review in abortion murder facilities. A physician could permanently injure many women without ever being called into accountability for poor medical practice. Hospitals and surgical centers require that a physician's work be reviewed routinely by other physicians who practice the same specialty. This is to help guarantee the *quality* of operations that are being performed. In every other medical setting, each surgeon must complete a questionnaire on complications for every patient receiving an operation.

Abortion clinics have no way to tell if there are complications or not! I heard an abortionist testify in Oregon that she did not have complications from her abortion procedures. An obstetrician and gynecologist in the Senate hearing room, had just testified about a patient he had treated who nearly died from an abortion. The injured patient was *that very abortion doctor's* patient. The abortionist had no way of knowing that there was a complication.

Breast Cancer

Abortion also places women at an increased risk for breast cancer. A comprehensive critical analysis review of sixty-one published studies on this topic was published in 1996, in the *Journal of Epidemiological Community Health,* from Hershey Medical Center by J. Brind, et. al. The authors concluded:

> The results support the inclusion of induced abortion among significant risk factors for breast cancer, regardless of parity or timing of abortion relative to the first term pregnancy. Although the increase in risk was relatively low, the high incidence of both breast cancer and induced abortion suggest a substantial impact of *thousands of excess cases per year currently,* and a potentially *much greater* impact in the next century, *as the first cohort of women exposed to legal induced abortion continues to age.*[8] (emphasis added)

Since over 40 percent of women have an abortion by the time they reach forty-five years of age,[9] we can expect the incidence of breast cancer to rise dramatically over the next twenty years.

One sad part of this statistic is that women are not being told the truth. If they knew the truth, many would act differently.

Complications in Later Pregnancies

The New York State Department of Health supported a study on pregnancies after abortions between 1975 and 1978. It documented the fact that women who were subjected to a prior abortion murder were *three times* more likely to have complications during labor. Dr. V. Logrillo et. al., published the results entitled, *Effect of Induced Abortion on Subsequent Reproductive Function.*[10] The same women were almost twice as likely to have a spontaneous fetal death of their subsequent wanted child; and, 40 percent more likely to have their born child die shortly after birth. We are beginning to see the fatal physical effects to women of our tolerance of abortion murder.

Post-Abortion Syndrome

Post-Abortion Syndrome has been recognized since 1981, when a mother who chose to have an abortion seven years earlier became interested in the psychological effects. Nancy Jo Mann interviewed thousands of women with psychological consequences of aborting their children. Dr. Vincent Rue and Dr. Susan Stanford-Rue treated thousands of these patients through their nonprofit group—Institute for Abortion Recovery and Research.

When asked if abortions are dangerous to a woman's mental health, Dr. C. Everett Koop, the former Surgeon General, replied, " There is no doubt about it." He tells of a case where the psychological consequences of the abortion murder were not known for ten years.

> A woman had a pregnancy at about 38 or 39 [years of age.] Her kids were teenagers. And without letting either her family or her husband know, she had an abortion. At the moment she said, "[The abortion was] the best thing that ever happened to me—clean slate, no one knows, I am all fine." Ten years later, she had a psychiatric break when one of those teenage daughters who had grown up, got married, gotten pregnant, delivered a baby, and presented it to her grandmother. . . . Unless you studied that one for ten years, you would say, "Perfectly fine result of an abortion."[11]

Clinical psychologist, Dr. Catherine A. Barnard, performed a study that was published in 1991 titled, "Stress Reactions in Women Related to Induced Abortion." The study demonstrated that 19 percent of post-abortion women were diagnosed with post-traumatic stress disorder. Nearly one-half of women suffered some type of emotional trauma as a result of the abortion.[12] These included sleep disorders and flashbacks of the abortion murder.

Women Exploited By Abortion (WEBA) was founded by Nancy Jo Mann. As President, she has spoken of the devastating effects of abortion on women as:

> Lowering of self-esteem. Preoccupation with death. Hostilities, self-destructive behavior, anger and rage. You can lose your temper quickly. A despair, helplessness, desire to remember the death date which is really weird but you do that.[13]

Psychiatric Problems

The *British Medical Journal* reported feelings of guilt, nervous disorders, sleeplessness and regret in "about half of all abortion patients."[14] These symptoms lasted *at least* eight weeks. Suicidal thoughts are not uncommon. In Cincinnati, Ohio, Suiciders Anonymous counseled 5,620 members in a thirty-five-month period. Over one-third were women who had abortions, and fourteen hundred were young women between 15 and 24-years-old who had abortions.[15] Do we really believe that abortion is for the mental health of the mother?

Most studies and polls do not diagnose Post-Abortion Syndrome—because they do not follow-up with the patients for a long enough period of time, or rely on inadequate questionnaires. A Canadian study performed a survey on women who had *previously denied* having any problem from their abortion procedure. One-half of these women were randomly selected to undergo psychotherapy.

> What emerged from psychotherapy was in sharp contrast [to the questionnaires], even when the woman had rationally considered abortion to be inevitable, the only course of action. . . . Although the outward appearance did not reveal it, there were deeper feelings "invariably of intense pain, involving bereavement and a sense of identification with the fetus."[16]

Post-abortion Syndrome is a serious problem for women who allow abortion murder to be committed upon their children.

Abortion—A Money Making Business

Abortion is a billion-dollar business. Abortionists love money more than women. This love of money is obvious when it comes to fetal tissue research, which continues to escalate. The University of Washington at Seattle opened an embryology laboratory, funded by the National Institute of Health. This NIH funded facility runs a round-the-clock collection service at abortion clinics. The dead babies are used to harvest body parts to help with research.

World magazine reported this shocking story: "Alan G. Fantel, Ph.D., of the University of Washington's Department of Pediatrics, wants to send you organs from unborn children killed at 'gestational ages between forty days and term.' You are reassured that these organs will be fresh."[17]

A price list for each part is provided—a liver is only one hundred and fifty dollars. I had difficulty believing this, so I checked the web myself. Sure enough, you may reach Dr. Fantel by calling his telephone number found on the web page advertising the fetal parts: http://grants.nih.gov/grants/guide/1994/94.03.11/notice-availability-003.html.

Since the intact fetus is worth more than one ripped apart by current abortion techniques, we can expect newer procedures that remove the baby alive and kill it as it exits the birth canal just as in partial birth abortions.

There are companies such as AGF which harvest fetal body parts and sell them to research facilities. Since the Uniform Anatomic Gift Act has made it a crime to sell parts, these companies merely charge to recover and transport them. AGF earned $2 million in 1998 for this type of business. Here is the evidence that women are not at the top of the priority list.

Conclusions

There are many feminists today who are pro-life. They recognize that the oppressor is joined to the oppressed. The uninformed mother has not been told the medical risks of abortion. Serious risks to the mother's life and health exist when women have an abortion. Prolonged psychological ill-effects of abortion are common.

The abortion industry makes billions of dollars on the murder of fetal humans. It pays to keep Americans uninformed. Pro-choice harms women. It is more loving to both baby *and mother* to protect human life from abortion murder.

People who vote pro-choice contribute to the killing of humans and to the physical and emotional harm of women. People who vote pro-life love their neighbor by trying to save them from death, and prevent women from suffering physical and psychological trauma. But, as we'll see next, a pro-choice vote endangers far more than women.

Notes

1. Anthony, S.B., *The Revolution* 4 (1): 4, 8 July 1869. Thanks to Coleen MacKay at Feminists for Life for confirming this quote on 11 February 2000.

2. Callahan, S., as quoted in "Susan B. Anthony: Pro-life Feminist," *Focus on the Family* (January 2000), 7.

3. Washington, B.T., "The Atlanta Exposition Address," *Up from Slavery* (Norwalk, CT: Easton Press, 1970), 147.

4. Bulfin, M. J., "Complications, deaths noted with abortions," *OB-GYN Observer* vol. 14, no. 6 (November 1975): 5.

5. Iffy, L., "Second Trimester Abortions," *Journal of the American Medical Association*, vol. 249, no. 5 (4 February 1983), 588.

6. See Appendix C.

7. *Planned Parenthood v. Casey*, 505 U.S. 833 (1983).8.

8. Brind, J., et. al., "Induced abortion as an independent risk factor for breast cancer: a comprehensive review and meta-analysis," *Journal of Epidemiological Community Health*, 1996.

9. Alan Guttamcher Institute, Abortion Facts, 1997.

10. Logrillo, V., et. al., *Effect of Induced Abortion on Subsequent Reproductive Function*, Contract #1-HD-6-2802, 1975-1978.

11. "Exclusive Interview: U.S. Surgeon General C. Everett Koop," *Rutherford Journal* (Spring 1989), 31.

12. Barnard, C.A., "Stress Reactions in Women Related to Induced Abortion," Association for Interdisciplinary Research in Values and Social Change, *Newsletter* (Winter 1991): 1-3.

13. Mann, N., "Women form WEBA to Fight Abortions," *The Washington Times* (3 August 1983).

14. Ashton, J.R., "The Psychological Outcome of Induces Abortion," *British Journal of Obstetrics and Gynecology* (December 1980): 1115-1122.

15. Uchtman, M., *Suicider's Anonymous Report to the Cincinnati City Council* (1981). Quoted in Wilke, J., *Abortion: Questions and Answers* (Cincinnati: Hayes Publishing Co, 1985), 125. The Ohio director of Suicider's Anonymous presented the report.

16. Editorial, "Psychological Sequelae of Therapeutic Abortion," *British Medical Journal* (May 1976): 1239.

17. Vincent, L., "The Harvest of Abortion," *World* (23 October 1999): 16-19.

10.

Pro-Choice: Does It Endanger Society?

During medical school at the University of Texas Medical Branch in 1979, I attended a film series by Francis Schaeffer and Dr. C. Everett Koop. These Christian men pressed the point that our recent acceptance of abortion would inevitably lead to euthanasia. I remember shaking my head and saying, "These guys are alarmists—that will never happen."

I was wrong. Oregon, where I live, was the first state in America to legalize physician-assisted suicide. Drs. Schaeffer and Koop could see something I could not. Abortion redefines, and then defies, the morals of any society.

The Indicator Sin

When environmentalists want to discover the health of an ecosystem in nature, they find an indicator species. The health of this species is an excellent indicator of the health of the entire system.

My friend, Tim Gilmer, says that abortion is an "indicator sin." The moral health of the nation may be revealed by our response to abortion. It seems that one famous nun agrees with Tim that our eco-society is in trouble. This is what Mother Teresa of Calcutta said in 1994:

> By abortion, the mother does not learn to love, but kills her own child to solve her problems. And by abortion, the father is told that he does not have to take any responsibility at all for the child he has brought into the world. That father is likely to put other women into the same trouble.

So abortion just leads to more abortion. Any country that accepts abortion is not teaching its people to love, but to use violence to get what they want.[1]

Since legalizing the killing of unborn children in 1973, we have seen the incidence of child abuse skyrocket 500 percent,[2] and we have witnessed with horror, numerous women killing their own born children.

Mothers Who Murder

The FBI reported in 1997 that five babies are killed every week in America. Between 250 and 300 infants have been killed yearly since 1991.[3]

How can we forget Susan Smith? This 23-year-old mother killed her two sons—a 3-year-old and a 14-month-old baby boy. She drowned them in her car as she rolled it into Long Lake in October 1994.[4]

Two teenage college freshmen, Amy Grossberg and Brian Peterson of New Jersey, killed their newborn with a blow to the head. This baby was left in a motel trash can in Delaware in 1996. The couple was charged with murder.[5]

A teenage mother in Pomona, California crushed the head of her 9-pound newborn baby. She then tossed the body over the fence to the neighbor's dogs.[6]

In Houston, Texas, the nation's fourth largest city, residents last year found thirteen newborn babies in trash bins and abandoned on doorsteps—all within a ten month period. Three of the babies were already dead. One 15-year-old mother was identified and charged with murder when her newborn daughter was found dead in a trash bin. The baby had allegedly died from blows to the head.[7]

Our nation was shocked by the most infamous high school prom in American history. High school student Melissa Drexler, delivered a healthy 6-pound 6-ounce baby boy in the restroom during the dance, placed him in the trash can, and left. She confessed the crime: "The baby was born alive. I knowingly took the baby out of the toilet and wrapped a series of garbage bags around the baby. I then knotted the garbage bag closed, and threw it in the trash can."[8] A person cleaning the restroom found blood, looked in the trash can, and discovered the dead baby—suffocated in the trash bags. Melissa was sentenced to fifteen years in prison for aggravated manslaughter.

Shocking or Expected?

Every one of these young people are only living out what they have been taught: "It is okay to kill your baby if you do not want it." For the past twenty-seven years, each mother could have had a legal abortion—up to the day prior to giving birth.

Our youth are smart enough to realize that there is no real difference in killing the baby in the womb or out of the womb. They are certainly acting more honestly than we are.

The multiple instances of teenagers committing murder in school shootings have us searching for explanations. Arkansas, Colorado, Georgia, Kentucky, Oregon, there are no limits. Human life is no longer sacred. One out of every four hospitalizations in Oregon in 1997 was suicide related (26 percent).[9] We are to blame. Legalizing the killing of innocent humans— who are made in God's image—has opened the floodgates of violence.

We contribute to these horrors by teaching our children that we descended from the animals by evolution—apart from God. Teach them that they are animals and they will most certainly act like animals. A book released this year by two scientists teaches that the rape of women is normal and "natural" by this same evolutionary thinking—animals do it.[10]

If we continue to teach children that killing a human is acceptable in one location (the womb) and not in another, they will despise our hypocrisy and continue to kill. But if we teach them that *all* human life is uniquely valuable—because we are made in the image of God—life becomes precious once again. Respect for human life then rests upon a solid philosophical foundation. Hypocrisy is unmasked by truth. *Then* we can expect the proper respect for human life to return to our children. For if our children do not change, then elderly parents will be next.

Euthanasia: Good Death?

The word *euthanasia* originates from two Greek forms—*eu* meaning "good" and *thanatos* meaning "death." Euthanasia is supposed to guarantee a "good death." Many Christians have been deceived by this terminology.

In a January 1999 research poll in Oregon, voters were asked the following question: "In the recent elections on the issue of assisted suicide in Oregon, did you favor or oppose assisted suicide?"[11] It was not surprising that 93 percent of non-Christians voted to legalize the killing of humans by physicians. But even the majority of Christians voted in favor of this form of euthanasia. The statistics reveal the particulars—mainstream Protestants 68 percent, Catholics 55 percent, and evangelicals 32 percent. Christians are confused.

There is a frightening similarity to Germany's euthanasia program. The killings began with fetuses and newborns and then progressed to the "humane" mercy killings of handicapped adults. The debilitated elderly were next in line to die. The geriatric killings were followed by whatever human group did not have a quality of life worth living. Of course, the government determined the arbitrary standard.

Euthanasia became popular after the publication of two books—Adolf Jost's, *The Right to Death* (1895), and *Permitting the Destruction of Life Not Worthy of Life* (1920). This latter book was written by two well-known men—Alfred Hoche, a prominent humanitarian medical doctor, and Karl Binding, a respected attorney.[12]

Medical doctors and German society supported and pushed for euthanasia—not Hitler. Relatives of infants with disabilities were requesting the government to end the drain on society. The first person killed by Hitler's regime was a handicapped child, baby Knauer, in 1938. The parents wanted the "useless eater" to be "put to sleep."[13]

We are marching in the same footsteps that led to the Holocaust of the Third Reich. "He's just an alarmist. It will never happen." That's what I thought when I heard Francis Schaeffer and C. Everett Koop.

Let's look at a country where the killings of humans occur *without* their consent—today.

Murder in the Netherlands

Physicians in the Netherlands practice euthanasia. They also practice killing their patients without that patient's consent. "Safeguards" have been in place since 1993, to assure that these physician-assisted suicides are done legally. But do they work?

Only 28 percent of Dutch physicians are honest about euthanasia killings when they fill out death certificates.[14] Over 41 percent have admitted to involuntary euthanasia.[15] A Dutch study, published in the *New England Journal of Medicine*, reported that 23 percent of doctors admitted having killed patients *without* that patient's explicit request.[16] "In the Netherlands, euthanasia and physician-assisted suicide have been practiced with increasing openness, although technically they remain illegal."[17] Isn't it interesting that these doctors are not punished?

In the Netherlands, even a nurse can now kill a patient in violation of the law without serious punishment. One nurse killed an AIDS patient; her sentence was two months probation.[18] Why stop with *physician*-assisted suicide? Any medically trained person can decide that you need to die.

Closer to Home

In Oregon, the supposed safeguards were bypassed in 1999, in the case of an elderly patient with cancer. When she requested physician-assisted suicide, her family physician sent her to a psychiatrist, as required by Oregon law.

The psychiatrist felt that she was cognitively impaired (similar to senile dementia) and, that her *daughter was pressuring her to end her life* by being "somewhat coercive." The irate daughter requested a second opinion. Who gave it? An HMO administrator approved the request for the mother to be killed. The daughter gave the pills to her mother and the elderly woman died that same day.[19]

Also in Oregon, an elderly man took his medicine to die, but the planned suicide went awry. The watching family called *911* because the symptoms were so disturbing. Paramedics rushed him by ambulance to a Portland hospital and revived him. When this was presented at a Portland Community Workshop on 3 December 1999, the director of Compassion in Dying Federation instructed one of the known anti-killing attendees not to tell the media. A Salem social worker confirmed the exchange.[20] A local radio program host, Lars Larson, discussed the incident on his show. The director dropped the phone and refused to talk anymore when confronted with a taped version of the report.

When the Oregon Health Division reported the 1999 physician-killing death statistics, neither of these two cases was mentioned.[21] When the government has embraced doctors killing their patients, and the public source of information places the Emperor's new clothes upon such violations of the Hippocratic Oath, the stage is set for far more than a mere fable for children. A true Shakespearean tragedy waits when no voice remains to cry that Juliet did not intend to die. The threads of euthanasia "safety controls" are not merely unraveling. In reality, such highly admired controls do not exist. We need an honest child to expose the naked truth of these imaginary safeguards from abuse.

When doctors are willing to violate natural law and their Hippocratic Oath, there remains no more restraint for the killing of undesirables by those in authority. Adolf Hitler did not begin the push for governmental killings; doctors and society pushed for these "needed" rights to end economic burdens.[22] Hitler only turned the direction of a fast-moving and popular idea to his own advantage.

Whether a dictatorship or a republic, danger lurks when those in power have a legal method of easing the economic burden of "undesirables." Have you noticed that more young people are seeing the elderly as an economic burden and undesirable? If I were elderly, I'd be fighting the euthanasia movement fiercely. I hope to be old one day, so I'm fighting it now!

The Netherlands is repeating the morbid history of Germany's past. We in America are running anxiously to join them. What appears to be a safe and painless answer to control our suffering, may turn out to be a gas chamber experience.

Suffering—The Ultimate Fear

Years ago, my wife and I had just watched the movie, *The Hiding Place*. As I considered the sacrifice that the ten Boom family made to love their Jewish neighbors in Nazi Germany, my emotions were raw. Then the sacrifice of Another came to mind.

> Who, in the days of flesh, when He had offered up prayers
> and supplications, with vehement cries and tears to Him
> [God the Father] who was able to save Him from death,
> and was heard in that He feared, though He was a Son, yet
> He learned obedience by the things which He suffered.
> (Heb. 5:7, 8)

This fact that even Jesus Christ had to suffer in order to learn obedience hit me afresh. So did Romans 8:17, which states plainly that we, also, must suffer in order to be glorified with Christ: ". . . And if children, then heirs—heirs of God and joint heirs with Christ, if indeed we suffer with Him, that we may also be glorified together" (Rom. 8:17).

That night as I put my 2-year-old daughter to bed, I was praying my usual request that she would become a godly person. But while praying, I began to cry uncontrollably—heaving soundlessly—out of deep pain. I had realized the full impact of this truth of suffering for the first time. I was asking that this baby girl whom I loved, lying innocently in her crib, would suffer.

For when I prayed that my little one would become godly, I was also asking God to allow her to suffer. Like Christ, that's how we become obedient—through our suffering.

The images of Corrie ten Boom and her sister flashed before me. Would my little girl be thrown in prison? Would she be raped? Would she be starved to death? Would they experiment on her? What else would she have to suffer for standing up for Jesus Christ? Only God knows the future. It is not a popular sermon or Bible study topic, but we Christians are called to suffer.

The Biblical View

Dr. Paul Fowler speaks powerfully on this neglected theme: "We live in a day when only two alternatives are considered: healing or death. We think, 'If I cannot be healed, then I want to die. Suffering is intolerable!' But suffering, in truth, is a biblical alternative."[23]

Pope John Paul II laments our present unbiblical view of suffering in his *Evangelium Vitae:*

... Those close to the sick person can be moved by an understandable, even if misplaced, compassion. All this is aggravated by a cultural climate which fails to perceive any meaning or value in suffering, but rather considers suffering the epitome of evil, to be eliminated at all costs.[24]

The Bible makes it clear that a person should not seek to be killed as an escape from suffering. In fact, one person who killed another person in the final moments of life was punished for murder.

That Joni Eareckson Tada is herself a quadriplegic, adds impact to her words on the subject.

The Old Testament records an incident involving King Saul of Israel, who became seriously wounded on the battlefield. Fearing the advancing enemy, Saul took his sword and tried to fall on it. He cried to a soldier, "Come and put me out of my misery for I am in terrible pain but life lingers on." The soldier deferred to the wishes of the king and killed him. Then acting most likely on his innocence, he brought some of Saul's armor to David and said, "I killed him, for I knew he couldn't live."

There were no laws on the books back then about assisted suicide, but that did not stop David from banging the gavel of Israel's justice. He ordered the soldier put to death. Perhaps onlookers were shocked by the verdict. After all, Saul was dying anyway, he was in great pain, and if captured, he feared torture and abuse in his final hours. These things were probably on the mind of the soldier who performed the mercy killing, but his actions stand in contrast with Saul's bodyguard who, minutes earlier, was too terrified to commit the act.[25] (2 Sam. 1:9-16; 1 Chron. 10:4)

Suffering should not be our greatest fear. When we have done all that we can do to prevent it within God's guidelines, we can trust God to use it for His purposes. It is only by suffering with Christ that we will be glorified together with Him.

Hope for the Dying

Terminal pain is a physically and emotionally devastating time for everyone involved, and sometimes seems unbearable.

When I was in medical school, I watched an intelligent, athletic, graduate student friend, diagnosed with Hodgkin's Disease (a type of cancer), slowly lose his strength. He was finally confined to a hospital bed where he could only whisper and think. He could not even feed or clean himself.

My friend was a good man, but he had never made peace with God. I could see that his time was near and that his pain was making it difficult to think. But, he kept hanging on, fighting to resolve something.

Another medical student and I went to his bedside to talk with him about God's grace provided in the death of Jesus Christ. The next day, he whispered to us that he had taken the necessary step to make peace with God. He died that night. Twenty years later, I still wear his necktie—beautifully decorated with a hand-embroidered pheasant. It reminds me of my friend and his struggle.

Fortunately, medical technology has increased dramatically since he died. Unfortunately, many people (including doctors) are not aware of these newer techniques to aid in dying.

"True compassion leads to sharing another's pain; it does not kill the person whose sufferings we cannot bear."[26]

Pain Control

As an orthopedic surgeon, I know that bone cancer can produce severe pain. Even this pain can be controlled with the proper techniques. Wesley J. Smith relates a story about this problem in his book, *Forced Exit*.

> Dr. Robin Bernhoft, a Washington surgeon, has seen such an effort succeed in his own family. That is one of the reasons he opposes euthanasia. Dr. Bernhoft told me the following story: "People who say bone cancer pain cannot be relieved are mistaken. My brother died of multiple myeloma [a bone marrow cancer] when he was forty-one. . . . It was as painful a case of cancer as I have seen since I became a surgeon in 1976. But Larry was lucky. He

was at the Mayo Clinic, where doctors knew how to take care of such horrible pain. Pain can almost always be controlled—and without putting people into a drugged stupor. Pain medicine—even morphine—goes straight to the pain. If the dosage is properly controlled, the patient will not feel drunk, drugged, and most importantly, will not be in pain.[27]

Although the Mayo Clinic is excellent, any metropolitan area now has doctors who can help even rural patients control their terminal pain. If you know someone who is suffering uncontrollable pain, be compassionate and find the right doctor.

Physicians for Compassionate Care is the national organization of medical doctors that promotes compassion in dying—without killing the patient. They support hospice care that offers a warm and compassionate alternative to dying in a cold hospital. Life does not need to be needlessly prolonged by the intervention of artificial technology. I belong to the Oregon chapter; it is the only position consistent with natural law, the Hippocratic Oath, and the protection of Americans from inevitable forced killings.

Conclusions

So, does voting pro-choice endanger society? You be the judge.

We have witnessed mothers killing their children by infanticide at alarming rates. We have proof in the Netherlands and Oregon that safeguards do not prevent abuse—involuntary killings still occur. We have read of the German experience. When medical doctors and society agree to kill undesirables for the betterment of society, a holocaust can occur.

Pain *can* be controlled at the end of life. Physician-assisted suicide is not the answer. Suffering is difficult, but necessary in God's plan. Killing a patient by euthanasia is *not* the compassionate choice.

Suffering should not be our greatest fear. Rather, our fear should be that Americans will choose the personal 'right' to euthanasia—at the expense of millions of future human deaths.

These deaths will be of the new undesirables—the unproductive elderly. Pro-choice endangers us all.

> Let those who seek death with dignity beware,
> lest they lose life with dignity in the process.[28]

C. Everett Koop, M.D.,
U.S. Surgeon General 1981-1989

Notes

1. Mother Teresa, "Whatsoever You Do," National Prayer Breakfast, Washington, D.C., 3 February 1994.

2. A 500 percent increase in the ten years after *Roe v. Wade*. The 1978 U.S. Department of Health, Education, and Welfare report entitled *1977 Analysis of Child Abuse and Neglect Research*. This was prior to the increased reporting twenty years later outlined by the U.S. Department of Health and Human Services Report; National Study on Child Abuse and Neglect Reporting, The American Humane Association, 1981 and 1991.

3. "Nearly five babies killed weekly, FBI data show, 27 June 1997," *CNN interactive*, accessed 21 January 2000, available from cnn.ch/US/9612/09/infant.death.indict/index.html.

4. "Susan Smith: Child Murderer or Victim?" The Crime Library, accessed 21 January 2000; available from www.crime-library.com/fiilicide/smith/3.htm.

5. "Teens indicted for first-degree murder in death of infant—9 December 1996," *CNN interactive*, accessed 21 January 2000, available from cnn.ch/US/9612/09/infant.death.indict/index.html.

6. "Mother Charged in Killing of Baby and Throwing Body to the Dogs," *Recent Horror Crimes*, accessed 21 January 2000; available from www.atps.com/crime/horror.htm.

7. Olasky, M., Ed., "Abortion by the numbers," *World* (22 January 2000): 26.

8. " 'Prom mom' admits killing newborn—20 August 1998," *CNN interactive*, accessed 21 January 2000; available from cnn.ch/US/9808/20/prom.birth.02.

9. *CD Summary,* Center for Disease Prevention and Epidemiology, Oregon Health Division, vol. 48, no. 18 (7 September 1999).

10. "Darwin Made Me Do It," *Breakpoint,* 1 February 2000; citing *A Natural History of Rape,* by Thornhill, R., and Craig T. Palmer.

11. "Impact of Abortion Views on Voting Decisions," Moore Information Public Opinion Research, 25 February 1999. Survey performed 21-22 January 1999.

12. Smith, W.J., *Forced Exit* (New York: Times Books, 1997), 73.

13. Ibid., 100.

14. van der Maas, P.J., "Euthanasia and Other Medical Decisions Concerning the End of Life," *Health Policy Monographs 2* (1992), 49.

15. Quoted in Smith, W.J., *Forced Exit,* 100, as reported by the Medicolegal Group of Limburg University in Maastricht.

16. van der Maas, P.J., et. al., "Euthanasia, Physician Assisted Suicide, and Other Medical Practices Involving the End of Life in the Netherlands, 1990-1995," *The New England Journal of Medicine* (November 1996), 335, 22:1699-1711. See also, Fenigsen, R., "Involuntary Euthanasia in Holland," *The Wall Street Journal* (30 September 1987).

17. Ibid., 1699.

18. "Dutch Court Rejects Nurse's Defense in Euthanasia Case," *Reuters,* 23 March 1995.

19. Barnett, E.H., "Is Mom Capable of Choosing to Die?," *The Oregonian* (17 October 1999): G1-2.

20. Baker, L., "Botched Suicide?" *Brainstorm,* accessed 24 February 2000; available from http://znetprime.znetsolutions..../ 493DCBB774E987F088 25688F002B6A71? Open Document.

21. Rojas-Burke, J., "Statistics put face on assisted suicide," *The Oregonian* (24 February 2000): 1. Also published in the *New England Journal of Medicine* of the same date.

22. Smith, W.J., *Forced Exit,* 77-80.

23. Fowler, P.B., *Abortion—Toward an Evangelical Consensus,* 128.

24. Pope John Paul II, *Evangelium Vitae 1995,* 695.

25. Tada, J.E., *WHEN IS IT RIGHT TO DIE?* (Grand Rapids, MI: Zondervan Publishing House, 1992), 111-112.

26. Pope John Paul II, *Evangelium Vitae 1995*, 713.

27. Smith, W.J., *Forced Exit*, 227.

28. Tada, J.E., *WHEN IS IT RIGHT TO DIE?*, in the foreword by C. Everett Koop, M.D.

God Is Love: So Don't Worry, Be Happy

Christianity has a unique place in the religions of the world. It is the only religion where a supreme God reaches down to help us humans—we, who cannot please God by our own efforts. The words of Jesus in John 3:16, capture His amazing love. "For God so loved the world that He gave His only born Son, that whoever believes in Him will not perish, but have everlasting life."

The Grace of God

Several decades ago, the theologians at Oxford were wrestling with the primary difference between Christianity and the other religions. When C.S. Lewis entered the room, they asked him his opinion of what makes Christianity unique from all other religions. C.S. Lewis answered succinctly, "That's easy—it's grace." Philip Yancey's book, *What's So Amazing about Grace*, reminds us of our need for the extravagant grace of our loving God.

> And then comes along a movie like *Forrest Gump*, about a kid with a low IQ who speaks in platitudes handed down from his mother. . . . Many thought it naïve, ridiculous, manipulative. Others, however, saw in it a rumor of grace that made a sharp relief against the violent ungrace of *Pulp Fiction* and *Natural Born Killers*. As a result, *Forrest Gump* became the most successful movie of its time. The world starves for grace.[1]

"Amazing Grace" remains one of the favorite hymns in the English language—perhaps because we all recognize, in those quiet moments, that only God's grace could "save a wretch like me." We Christians have truly been blessed with God's amazing grace. Only God could have come up with such an incredible plan to save us from our own sinfulness.

Philip Yancey also reminds us of the grace of Mother Teresa:

> We are inconsistent, said Mother Teresa, to care about violence, and to care about hungry children in places like India and Africa, and yet not care about the millions who are killed by the deliberate choice of their own mothers. She proposed a solution for those pregnant women who don't want their children: "Give that child to me. I want it. I will care for it. I am willing to accept any child who would be aborted and to give that child to a married couple who will love the child and be loved by the child."[2]

Suddenly, we realize a tension. A woman of grace and a man writing about this grace, bring to our attention a problem. Mother Teresa has pricked our consciences with the issue of abortion. Although God is both perfect and gracious, we sinners are not. Sin causes injustice and even death. How do we find grace in her statement "killed by the deliberate choice of their own mothers"?

God Is Love

Pope Paul II has spoken to this in his *Encyclical, The Gospel of Life.*

> I would now like to say a special word to women who have had an abortion. The church is aware of the many factors which may have influenced your decision, and she does not doubt that in many cases it was a painful and even shattering decision. The wound in your heart may not yet have healed. Certainly what happened was and remains terribly wrong. But do not give in to discouragement and do not lose hope. Try rather to understand what happened and face it honestly. If you have not already done so, give yourselves over with humility and trust to repentance. The Father of mercies is ready to give you his forgiveness and

his peace in the sacrament of reconciliation. You will come
to understand that nothing is definitively lost, and you will
also be able to ask forgiveness from your child, who is now
living in the Lord.[3]

The Holy Scriptures make God's forgiveness clear in I
John 1:9, "If we confess our sins, He is faithful and just to
forgive us our sins, and to cleanse us from all unrighteousness."
Repentance and confession bring pardon and forgiveness. This
is the message of the gospel—God's grace offers forgiveness.
This forgiving grace is the message in Jesus' parable of the
Prodigal Son.

In Luke 15, Jesus unfolds what many consider to be the
best short story ever told. A young man dishonors his father by
asking for his inheritance *before* the father had died. The young
man rashly takes the money and wastes it in sinful behavior in
another country. After losing it all, he is forced to feed pigs in
order to keep himself alive. As he looks down at the muck of
manure and rotting food at his feet, he begins to see things
more clearly. He will return to his father and confess his sin.
He will ask to be a hired servant.

But as he nears his home, the father who has been earnestly
watching for a long time, sees him coming. The elderly father
literally runs to welcome his son. A lavish banquet is prepared
to celebrate the return of this lost son. Why? The son is still a
son—not a servant. The grace and mercy of God shout loud and
clear that repentance and confession bring pardon and forgiveness.

In the beauty of this grace, one element is often forgotten.
The inheritance that was given to this son was forever lost. It
was wasted—the money, the time, the relationships, and the
opportunities to help the father. Similarly, the relationship with
our Father may be restored for eternal enjoyment. But the
reward and privileges of serving together in the family are lost.
Even repentance cannot bring back the missed opportunities to
serve, and to suffer with Christ, which results in reward.

Hebrews 12:16-17 speaks of this in relation to Esau:

> Lest there be any fornicator (sexual sin) or profane person
> like Esau, who for one morsel of food sold his birthright,
> for you know that afterward, when he wanted to inherit the

blessing, he was rejected, for he found no place for repentance, though he sought it diligently with tears.

Eternal life was not the question. The question was God's temporal blessing here on earth. The blessing of God as the leader of the family line had been lost—it could not be regained—even with sincere repentance.

This concept may also be found in Romans 8:17.

The Spirit Himself bears witness with our spirit that we are the children of God, and if children then heirs—heirs of God; and, joint heirs with Christ if indeed we suffer with Him that we may also be glorified together.

We are children of God if we have accepted Christ's sacrifice on our behalf. But we are co-heirs with Christ only if we suffer faithfully with Him. The one inheritance is by grace alone. The other comes through grace but necessitates our faithfulness in suffering. God will remain our Father, but the missed opportunity to serve Christ results in a permanent loss of reward. God's grace and love for His children does not allow Him to let them run wild—there are consequences.

The Goal of the Christian

When Christians are asked about the goal of life, many will respond "to be with God in heaven." Now, it is true that we will be in heaven with God. But, I would suggest that God's goal for us is actually much more specific. Max Lucado alludes to this goal in his book, *Just Like Jesus*:

Can you think of a greater gift than to be like Jesus? Christ felt no guilt; God wants to banish yours. Jesus had no bad habits; God wants to remove yours. Jesus had no fear of death; God wants you to be fearless. Jesus had kindness for the diseased and mercy for the rebellious and courage for the challenged. God wants you to have the same. God loves you just the way you are, but He refuses to leave you that way. He wants you to be just like Jesus.[4]

God has made this goal clear in Romans 8:29, "For whom He foreknew, He also predestined to be conformed to the image of His Son." In John's epistle, we read, "Beloved, now we are the children of God; and it has not yet been revealed what we shall be, but we know that when He is revealed, we shall be like Him, for we shall see him just as He is" (1 John 3:2). What is God's goal for us? It is for us to become *Just Like Jesus*.

This goal *will* be reached, after we die. However, God desires us to become more like Jesus here on earth. This can be found in St. Paul's letter to the church at Thessalonica. "For this is the will of God, your sanctification: that you should abstain from sexual immorality; that each one of you should know how to possess his own vessel in sanctification and honor" (1 Thess. 4:3).

The word *sanctification* beautifully illustrates God's desire for us. It means "to set apart as holy unto God." It has the concept of setting it aside as special. God views us as the finest china pulled out of storage for a banquet of the Greatest King. He did not intend for us to take ourselves outside to the sandbox for childish play. This vessel of fine china—this physical body that we have been given—should be set apart for God. The sandbox of sin is for immature children: We are like fine china destined for the King's banquet table.

If we play in the sandbox of sin, He will make us clean through the washing of His Spirit. We will be clean when we see Him. But if we have been chipped through play, we may not be placed for use on His table. This is where grace and responsibility can be seen side by side. If we do not pursue this holiness, we lose out on a wonderful opportunity. God expects us to be holy, like He is holy.

The Apostle Peter wrote, "but as He who called you is holy, you be holy in all your conduct, because it is written, 'Be holy, for I am holy' " (1 Pet. 1:16).

The Holiness of God

One day I was studying my Greek New Testament in seminary. My Greek language skills were quite basic. As I interpreted two Greek words (*Pneumati Hagioi*) my mind reverted back to a beginner's literal translation—"Spirit of Holy." This, of course, should be translated as the "Holy Spirit." As I pondered my mistake, the heavens opened, and I realized a truth that I had never seen. God Himself gave us the name of His

Spirit. He did not call Himself, the Grace Spirit, Merciful Spirit, Omnipotent Spirit, or Omniscient Spirit. He called Himself the *Holy* Spirit.

The chief attribute of God, which separates God from man, is His Holiness. It is sin that separates us from Him—not our finite bodies or minds. R.C. Sproul has written a book entitled, *The Holiness of God,* because "The one concept, the central idea I kept meeting in Scripture, was the idea that God is *holy.* . . . Only once in sacred Scripture is an attribute of God elevated to the third degree. Only once is a characteristic of God mentioned three times in succession."[5]

In a story about his training, Dr. Sproul confesses his own struggle with grace and God's holiness.

> At the end of my sermon the professor had a question for me. "Mr. Sproul," he said, "where did you get the idea that God's grace is infinite? Is there absolutely no limit to His grace?" As soon as he asked me that question, I knew I was in trouble. I could quote him chapter and verse of the hymn that taught me that, but somehow I couldn't come up with a single Scripture verse that taught God's grace is infinite.
>
> The reason I couldn't find any Scripture passage to support my statement is because there is none. God's grace is not infinite. God is infinite, and God is gracious. We experience the grace of an infinite God, but grace is not infinite. God sets limits to His patience and forbearance. He warns us over and over again that someday the ax will fall and His judgment will be poured out.[6]

Ouch! Now we have introduced another aspect to this concept of grace—it is not infinite. God does hold us accountable. How can a God who is love also punish us?

For those of us who are parents, we need only look at our children to find the answer. Love without disciplining punishment results in spoiled children; or worse, it results in children who cannot respond properly to authority—troublemakers, lawbreakers, and even violent children. Discipline here on earth is God's method of encouraging us to become like Jesus—to obey His commandments.

Conclusions

The view of God as "only love" must be balanced with the biblical presentation of His character. God is also holy—this is His primary attribute that separates Him from man. Our goal is to become like Jesus.

Many of us see Jesus as a gentle, kind, and loving man, holding children in His arms. He would never speak ill of anyone and offers only love. But this view does not do justice to the apostles who recorded His words and actions. The holiness of God does not allow Him to overlook our sin—especially one as serious as killing those made in His image.

In the next chapter, we will meet the Jesus about whom we were never taught.

Notes

1. Yancey, P., *What's So Amazing About Grace?* (Grand Rapids: Zondervan Publishing House, 1997), 40.

2. Ibid., 245.

3. Pope John Paul II, *Evangelium Vitae 1995*.

4. Lucado, M., *Just Like Jesus* (Nashville, TN: Word Publishing, 1998), Cover.

5. Sproul, R.C., *The Holiness of God*, 12, 26.

6. Ibid., 128-129.

Bad News: Sin and Judgment

Many Christians appear unconcerned about standing before God—after all, God is love. They know the *good* news—God is love—because most churches model it.

But the bad news is this: the majority of Americans do not know about God's holiness and wrath. Forty-four percent of us believe that "all people will experience the same outcome after death, regardless of their religious beliefs."[1] "Two out of three born-again believers assert there is no such thing as absolute truth."[2]

George Barna quotes more sad statistics: the average Christian spends more time watching television in one evening than he or she spends reading the Bible during the entire week (Ibid). He then tells us why churches cannot be unified.

> First it affects church unity. When we claim to be followers of Christ but lack a biblical view of reality, the Church itself cannot be unified. Without a worldview shaped by the Bible, our efforts are, by default, shaped by the subjective and conflicting standards of other organizations, groups, and systems. (Ibid)

So, let's take a look at a Jesus who rarely receives any press coverage—even in Church.

The Jesus We Never Knew

Jesus did say, "turn the other cheek" (Luke 6:29). He also turned over tables, threw business people's money around the temple, and made a whip to drive animals out of God's temple (John 2:15). He warns of judgment if repentance does not occur. "Repent, or else I will come to you quickly and will fight against them with the sword of my mouth" (Rev. 2:16).

Jesus told the woman caught in adultery, "Neither do I condemn you." But he also said, "Go and sin no more" (John 8:11). This should be seen in light of His comment to the lame man whom He healed at the pool of Bethesda. "See, you have been made well; sin no more, lest a worse thing come upon you" (John 5:14). In Revelation 3:16, we find a balancing of God's love of John 3:16: "I will vomit you out of my mouth."[3]

This Jesus of love called people hypocrites and fools (Luke 11:40,44). He warned of judgment: "Or those eighteen on whom the tower in Siloam fell and killed them, do you think that they were worse sinners than all other men who dwelt in Jerusalem? I tell you, no; but unless you repent you will all likewise perish" (Luke 13:4-5).

As Albert Schweitzer, a biblical scholar, who became famous as a medical missionary to Africa, wrote, "Scholars looked down the well of history and mistook their own reflection for the historical Jesus."[4] We must not overlook the full gospel according to Jesus. To confine Jesus to grace and forgiveness is to paint a caricature of Him.

The Apostle Paul has written in Romans 1:18, "For the wrath of God is revealed from heaven against all ungodliness and unrighteousness of men, who suppress the truth in unrighteousness." R.C. Sproul correctly concludes, "But a loving God who has no wrath is no God. He is an idol of our own making as much as if we carved Him out of stone."[5]

We must resist the temptation to make God in our own image. The God of the Bible (both New Testament and Old Testament—both God the Father and God the Son) characterizes grace, love, and forgiveness—balanced with His primary attribute of Holiness. Therefore, He must be a God of wrath against sin and a God who will judge. Any other view of God sets us up for a very unpleasant surprise when we meet Him.

I must confess that I had an incomplete view of God when I was younger. Some of the Christians around me quoted verses such as Psalms 103:12: "As far as the east is from the west, so far has He removed our transgressions from us." This was followed by John 5:24, "Most assuredly, I say to you, he who hears my word and believes in Him who sent me has everlasting life, and will not come into judgment, but has passed from death into life."

A favorite was Jeremiah 31:34—"for I will forgive their iniquity and I will remember their sin no more." The context is God's new covenant with the house of Israel, whose sin was no longer going to result in temporal judgment (Jer. 31:27-32). This verse and the ones prior do not teach that a Christian need never worry again about standing before God in judgment.

Verses such as 2 Corinthians 5:10 and Colossians 3:24-25 make this evident:

> We are confident, yes, well pleased rather to be absent from the body (physically dead) and to be present with the Lord. . . . Therefore, we make it our aim, whether present or absent, to be well pleasing to Him. For we must all appear before the judgment seat of Christ, that each one of us may receive the things done in the body, according to what he has done, whether good or bad. Knowing therefore the terror of the Lord, we persuade men. [And] Knowing that from the Lord you will receive the reward of your inheritance; for you serve the Lord Christ. But he who does what is wrong will be repaid for what he has done, and there is no partiality.

Many theologians would view these verses as a warning about "false Christians" who merely profess to believe in Christ, while their actions prove they are not really Christians. Others see them as only for true Christians who have already died. In this view, the judgment seat of Christ determines additional eternal rewards—a separate judgment from the one that determines eternal life.[6, 7] Regardless of the view taken, the point is clear. God's grace must be balanced with God's judgment.

Does God Punish Sin?

At this point, some of you are asking the right question. *What in the world does this have to do with abortion, euthanasia, and voting?* I felt a need to include this theological primer for this reason: We live in an age where God is no longer viewed as a God who will punish sin. If God does not punish sin, then who cares if abortion and voting are sin?

The famous Russian author of the 1800s, Fyodor Dostoevsky, wrote about this in *The Brothers Karamazov*. According to Sigmund Freud, it is the most magnificent novel ever written.

> There must be no more of this, monks, no more torturing children, rise up and preach that, make haste, make haste! God will save Russia, for though the masses are corrupted and cannot renounce their filthy sin, yet they know it is cursed by God and that they do wrong in sinning. So that our people still believe in righteousness, have faith in God and weep tears of devotion. It is different with the upper classes. They, following science, want to be a just social order on reason alone, without the help of Christ, as before, and they have already proclaimed that there is no crime, that there is no sin. And that is consistent, for if you have no God, what is the meaning of crime?[8]

So, there are two ways to sin freely without fear. One is a reductionist argument that reduces God's character to love—He will not punish sin. This ultimately leads to Universalism. This false religion claims that God will save everyone, so that none are punished. Why? God overlooks sin. If this is true, God committed the ultimate sin of injustice by forcing Jesus Christ to die as a sacrifice for our sin (that He would have overlooked anyway.) Although Christ died so that all might be saved, not all will be in heaven with Him (Rev. 21:8).

Jesus tells us a story—perhaps not a parable—in Luke 16 of the rich man and Lazarus. Since He never used real names in His parables, these may represent recently deceased people. Jesus makes clear that the rich man cried out in torment, "have mercy on me, and send Lazarus, that he may dip the tip of his finger in water and cool my tongue; for I am tormented in this flame." Jesus does not seem to indicate that everyone will be enjoying the beauty of heavenly bliss.

The second way to sin freely without fear is this: change God's absolute standards into arbitrary suggestions or cultural anachronisms. Satan is a master at this technique, as John Milton relates in 1664. This section of *Paradise Lost* tells of Satan's

discussion with Eve about the benefits of the forbidden tree—
the plant of knowledge of good and evil:

> The Tempter, all impassioned, thus began:
>
> O sacred, wise, and wisdom giving Plant,
>
> Mother of Science! Now I feel thy power
>
> Within me clear, not only to discern
>
> Things in their causes, but to trace the ways
>
> Of highest agents, deemed however wise.
>
> Queen of this Universe! Do not believe
>
> Those rigid threats of death; ye shall not die.
>
> How should ye? By the fruit? It gives you life
>
> To knowledge; by the Threatener? Look on me,
>
> Me who have touched and tasted, yet both live,
>
> And life more perfect have attained by Fate
>
> Meant me, by venturing higher than my lot.
>
> Shall that be shut to Man which to the beast
>
> Is open? Or will God increase his ire
>
> For such a petty trespass, and not praise
>
> Rather your vauntless virtue, whom the pain
>
> Of death denounced, whatever thing Death be,
>
> Deterred not from achieving what might lead
>
> To happier life, knowledge of good and evil?
>
> Of good, how just? Of evil—if what is evil
>
> Be real, why not known, since easier shunned?
>
> God, therefore, cannot hurt ye, and be just;
>
> Not just, not God; not feared then, not obeyed.[9]

Milton also had a grasp of the *result* of such a denial of
God's punishment of sin. This Holy God commands Michael
the Archangel,

Haste thee and from the Paradise of God

without remorse drive out the sinful pair,

From hallowed ground th' unholy, and denounce

To them, and to their progeny, from thence

Perpetual banishment. Yet, lest they faint

At the sad sentence rigorously urged. [10]

Jesus tells us at His trial before Pontius Pilate, that some sins are more serious than others. He answers Pilate in John 19:11: "therefore, the one that delivered Me to you has the greater sin."

Jesus Himself will punish sin as seen in multiple warnings in Revelation 2 and 3.

> Repent, or else I will come to you quickly and fight against them with the sword of my mouth. . . . So then, because you are lukewarm, and neither cold nor hot, I will vomit you out of my mouth. Because you say, "I am rich, have become wealthy, and have need of nothing"—and do not know that you are wretched, miserable, poor, and naked. (Rev. 2:15, 3:16-17)

To be spiritually poor and naked before God is a sobering thought. The holiness of God is ever so much as real as the grace of God. The wrath of God receives equal billing with the mercy of God. Unless we are able to see this biblical principle clearly, it will allow us to succumb to the same temptation as Adam and Eve—and, with the same tragic results. God does indeed punish sin.

What Is Truth?

Remember George Barna's sobering statistic about two-thirds of Christians not believing in absolute truth? He defines Christians as—"people who say they have made a personal commitment to Jesus Christ that is still important in their life today and whom claim that after they die they will go to heaven because they have confessed their sins and accepted Jesus Christ as their Savior."[11]

Upon what do those Christians base their claim to eternal life? If there is no absolute moral truth, then the Bible does not contain it. It is full of ideas and suggestions—not God's absolutes. If we cannot rely upon the Bible to find God's absolute truth on moral issues, then the Bible is no different than my daily newspaper or an archaic book of stories.

If this Book on spirituality does not contain absolute truth on morals, why should we believe *anything* in it? We should not. For then, our "hope is built on nothing less" than wishful dreams of happiness.

Dennis McCallum laments this tragedy in his book, *The Death of Truth*. He quotes a column in *Dear Abby* where Abby writes, "In my view, the height of arrogance is to attempt to show people the errors in the religion of their choice."[12]

> Abby implies that because a person has chosen a religion, others should accept its validity without assessment . . . according to post-modernists, people "construct" reality—that is, something is true *because* I believe it. Therefore, by challenging the truth claims of another's religion, we devalue the person, who is the source of his or her own truth . . . In place of truths that make sense or truths that can be backed up in some way, post-modernism again leaves its adherents with two things: experience and power. My experience is the basis for my beliefs, and those beliefs exist to empower me.[13]

We Christians appear to have climbed aboard the thinking of the world—a pagan society traveling at light speed to a post-modernist black hole. This very Jesus whom we claim to have received as Savior reprimands such misguided thinking.

Jesus launched stellar attacks on the religious leaders of His day. He accused them of practicing a wrong religion, as He spoke with absolute truth—the One who had authority to speak absolutely. Matthew 7:28-29 records, "when Jesus had ended these sayings, that the people were astonished at His teachings, for He taught them as one having authority, and not as the scribes." Jesus' words were strong:

> Woe unto you scribes and Pharisees, hypocrites! For you pay tithe of mint and anise and cumin, and have neglected

the weightier matters of the law: justice and mercy and
faith. These you ought to have done, without leaving the
others undone. Blind guides, who strain at a gnat and
swallow a camel. . . . Woe unto you, scribes and Pharisees,
hypocrites! For you are like whitewashed tombs which
indeed appear beautiful outwardly, but inside are full of
dead men's bones and all uncleanness. (Matt. 23:23-27)

Jesus does not sound like a post-modernist. His teaching
and strong rebukes reveal a foundation of absolute truth. He
was not afraid to tell others that their religion was wrong. Jesus
also said, "I am the way, the truth, and the life. No one comes
to the Father except through me" (John 14:6). "Heaven and
earth will pass away, but My words will by no means pass away"
(Matt. 24:35). Jesus prays to God the Father, "They are not of
the world, just as I am not of the world. Sanctify them by Your
truth. Your word is truth" (John 17:16-17).

God's Word is truth—absolute truth. The Bible contains
the moral absolutes by which Jesus Himself warns that we will
be judged. "He who rejects Me, and does not receive My words,
has that which judges him—the word that I have spoken will
judge him in the last day" (John 12:48).

Jesus also said, "Therefore, whoever hears these sayings of
mine, and does them, I will liken him to a wise man who built
his house upon a rock" (Matt. 7:24). "I have come that they
may have life and that they may have it more abundantly" (John
10:10). God does desire for us to have a wonderful life of
enjoyment. (This does not mean that there will be no difficul-
ties.) God guarantees that we can enjoy knowing Him; and,
have a successful life by obeying His commandments.

Conclusions

The lack of unity among Christians is in large part due to
biblical illiteracy. We are soaking in the pollution of a pagan
world's message instead of God's message.

Jesus cannot be reduced to a kind man. God cannot be
placed in the box of love. Both God the Father and God the
Son will judge sternly according to the absolute commands and
principles clearly spoken in the Holy Scriptures.

To play instead of preparing for difficult final exams, is foolish in educational training. In spiritual training for eternity, the consequences of such wrong priorities may be disastrous.

Only a biblical view of God will result in passing His exams. God has spoken absolute truth. God will punish sin. God has a holy wrath that prohibits Him from ignoring or overlooking sin. He is a God of judgment, as well as a God of amazing grace and forgiveness.

In the words of Emily Dickinson:

'Twas a long time parting, but the time

For interview had come;

Before the judgment seat of God,

The last and second time.[14]

With this in mind, let's take a look more specifically at God's priorities in voting.

Notes

1. Barna, G., *The Second Coming of the Church*, 21.

2. Ibid., 123.

3. Terry, R.A., *Why Does a Nice Guy Like Me . . . Keep Getting Thrown in Jail?* (Lafayette, LA: Huntington House Publishers, 1993), 103. Terry makes these same points.

4. Schweitzer, A., *The Quest of the Historical Jesus* (New York: MacMillan Publishing Co., 1968). This quote is attributed to Schweitzer, although I was unable to find the exact source. It certainly summarizes his brilliant book in both content and style as evidenced by this quote on page 325. "Men who have no qualifications for the task, whose ignorance is nothing less than criminal, who loftily anathematize scientific theology instead of making themselves in some measure acquainted with the researches which it has carried out, feel impelled to write a Life of Jesus, in order to set forth their general religious view in a portrait of Jesus which has not the faintest claim to be historical, and the most farfetched of these find favor, and are eagerly absorbed by the multitude."

5. Sproul, R.C., *The Holiness of God*, 179.

6. Lutzer, E.W., *Your Eternal Reward* (Chicago, IL: Moody Press, 1998).

7. Wilkin, R., *Confident in Christ* (Irving, TX: Grace Evangelical Society, 1999).

8. Dostoevsky, F., *The Brothers Karamazov* (Norwalk, CT: Easton Publications, 1979), 241.

9. Milton, J., *Paradise Lost* (Norwalk, CT: The Easton Press, 1976), 9:219-220.

10. Ibid., 11:270.

11. Barna, G., *The Second Coming of the Church,* 123.

12. McCallum, D., *The Death of Truth* (Minneapolis, MN: Bethany House Publishers, 1996), 200.

13. Ibid., 202.

14. Dickinson, E., *Poems of Emily Dickinson* (Norwalk, CT: The Easton Press, 1980), 40.

13.

Voting: God's Priority

The lordship of Christ extends to every area of our lives—
that includes voting.

But what is a vote for life? How do we determine if a
candidate shares God's priority? Is it always a sin to vote for a
pro-choice candidate?

Is Pro-Choice Always Sin?

God calls us to be people of principle who know what we
believe, why we believe it, and who will not compromise His
Scriptures. I have a close friend who is a person of principle. I
enjoy talking with her. She once made the comment that she
would never vote for a candidate who was not pro-life. Why?
Voting pro-choice is a sin.

Initially, I thought her stand on principle might be correct.
But I began to ask other Christians whom I knew to be knowl-
edgeable in this area: is it *always* sin to vote for a pro-choice
candidate? Or, is there sometimes a greater principle that is
more honoring to God?

First, I had to answer another question. What is God's
attitude toward the way in which we vote? We can be sure that
God holds us responsible for each vote. Life and death issues
are at stake. I believe that God holds us responsible for making
the best choice—that is, to do the greatest good. God's greatest
priority of good, as we saw previously, is to save innocent human life.

If we stand behind a candidate who votes to save the lives
of innocent humans, then we share in the reward. But stand
behind a pro-choice (to allow the killing of humans and harm
women) candidate, and we share in the judgment. So what

about voting when one candidate votes to save the lives of some humans, when the only other candidate would save none?

Ron Norquist, of Eternal Perspectives Ministries, reminds us that President Bush was against abortion in all cases except rape and incest. That would have stopped over 95 percent of all unborn human murders. Almost all of the 1.5 million murdered humans in each of those years would have been saved.

His opponent, Bill Clinton, favored abortion in every case throughout the ninth month of pregnancy—eventually even the gruesome partial birth abortions. Although Norquist did not favor allowing the killing of humans from rape or incest, he voted for George Bush because he could save more innocent humans.[1]

He chose the greater good in order *to save as many lives as possible*. This is far different than choosing the lesser of two evils. There is a conscious choice for God's highest good among persons in society.

Voting Priority Verses Principle

Some Christians believe that it's always wrong to vote for a pro-choice candidate. I understand their position. I held this position myself for a time.

These Christians should *not* violate their conscience.[2] People who know me can verify my uncompromising stand on principles. But in this case, there are innocent lives at stake. If I can even save some of those children, it will be better than saving none. My conscience can be clear because my goal has been both biblical and consistent—I've helped save as many human lives as possible. I would appeal to the conscience of my principled brothers and sisters by asking a similar question. Is it better to save no children or to save some children?

Many Christians still vote from an "exclusive principle." They exclusively vote *only* for a person who favors the ban of abortion in all cases, except to save the life of the mother. The principle is correct—the priority is wrong. Are we really willing to allow 95 percent of millions of babies to die because we cannot save every one of them?

Principles must match priorities. Our priority is to save as many lives as possible right now. To allow nine to die until we can save all ten is unthinkable.

Even when there is no true pro-life candidate, a vote is required that upholds God's value of human life. For example, if there were two pro-choice (to kill humans and harm women) candidates, but one opposed euthanasia and physician-assisted suicide, wouldn't it be better to try to save the lives of *some* humans rather than not vote as a matter of principle? Our compelling interest is the saving of *as many human lives* as possible.

Therefore, it is *not always* sin to vote for a pro-choice candidate. If we apply the principle of highest good—saving as many human lives as possible—we could vote for a pro-choice candidate without sinning. In fact, *not to vote* to save those lives is a sin.

What if a candidate who appeared pro-life later does something to harm life? If we cast a vote in good faith for the best pro-life candidate from available information, we have not sinned. The vote was cast in obedience to God's priority of saving human life. The candidate is then responsible to God.

Who Is A Pro-Life Candidate?

A pro-life candidate is one who understands that abortion, euthanasia, physician-assisted suicide, and infanticide are *all* morally wrong for society. These are all murder and, therefore morally wrong by either natural law, or by biblical command or principle.

A pro-life person doesn't believe that these murders of human life can be pigeonholed as being "personally opposed to abortion." (We'll look at this in detail later in this chapter.)

This was God's first law for society and the first role of government ordained by God. Our American *Declaration of Independence* declares that the right to life is the first unalienable right endowed by our Creator to us humans. It *must* be the government's role to protect innocent human life. A pro-life candidate stands for these God-given rights.

A pro-life candidate understands that there are extremely rare cases where a mother's life is at risk from pregnancy. Rarely, a medical procedure must be performed to save the life of the mother, realizing that the child in her womb may die as a result.

The Mother's Life

Betty Anderson, President of Christian Coalition in Montgomery County, Texas, says, "We are unapologetically pro-life and believe that life begins at conception, but that doesn't mean that we are in favor of endangering the life of the mother."[3]

With medical advances, there are only two instances where the life of the mother is at risk. One is ectopic pregnancy where the fetus is growing within the fallopian tube—outside of the womb. The tube will inevitably rupture, resulting in a true medical emergency. Two friends of mine have experienced this frightening emergency. The mother can lose her life from blood loss very quickly.

The child is already dead. In this case, the tube must be removed. Unfortunately, due to rampant premarital sex and sexual diseases, ectopic pregnancies have increased. In fact, in the twenty-two years since abortion on demand was legalized, the Center for Disease Control reported a 600 percent increase in ectopic pregnancies.[4]

The second type of case is cancer—particularly of the uterus. An Oregon mother was delighted to learn that she was pregnant until she was told the same day that she had cancer. If her treatment were delayed, it would put her life at risk. However, the same treatment might kill the child inside her. This 36-year-old mother determined to carry her children (yes, she had twins) to term—even at the risk of dying. Barbara Barton delivered a healthy boy and girl, but died six months later from a complication of her cancer treatment. She never regretted her decision.[5]

There was a couple in a church who suffered an emotional crisis when Pam was diagnosed with a rare cancer. Pam was also pregnant. Her husband pressed for an abortion because the chemotherapy could severely injure the child. Pam did not have the abortion although she had undergone a course of chemotherapy. Today, this wonderful couple is proud of their 19-year-old daughter who is intelligent and without deformity.

Rarely, medical treatment of the mother does result in the abortion of a child. If the child is not killed intentionally, this is not a direct abortion. Preserving the life of the mother is the pro-life position.

Deceit: Health and Personally Opposed

In contrast, to claim that abortion may be performed for the *health* of the mother is political deceit. Mental health has been expanded to include every conceivable case where a mother desires to kill her child.

Shifting from *life* of the mother to *health* of the mother occurred in *Doe v. Bolton* in 1973.[6] In this case from Georgia, the state law had previously allowed abortions for medical necessity, rape, incest, and fetal abnormality.* Health was not included—mental health in particular. The Supreme Court determined that "health" could be interpreted as anything to help the mother mentally. Avoiding the inconvenience of carrying her child to term would benefit the mother's mental health.

What had previously been a few thousand abortions per year, suddenly opened into a flood of abortions to kill our unborn neighbors—1.5 million per year. "Health of the mother" is *purposely* vague and deceitful. It must be removed from the law of our land. By using the same semantic deception, adult murders may be justified. Perhaps we should legalize first-degree murder among adults for the "health of the murderer." Adult murder would also be rampant if we legalized it for "health."

Protecting *the life* of the mother is *essential*. Protecting *the health* of the mother presently results in 1.3 million murders each year.

What if a candidate claims, "I am *personally* opposed to abortion. However, I believe that a woman should have the right to choose."

That's like saying, "I am personally opposed to murder. However, if a woman wants to murder another woman, then she should have the right to choose to murder." What kind of personal conviction is that? This misguided idea of "personal opposition" can be based on the post-modern corruption that values are not absolute—what is morally wrong for me may not be wrong for you. Or it may be a political smoke screen to lull those who are easily deceived. The taking of innocent human life

---

*Note that a handicapped person had already been demoted to subhuman status.

is wrong for *all* people of *all* societies at *all* times in history. We are to commit ourselves to save innocent human life universally.

Dr. Robert George clarifies the foolishness of such a personally opposed position:

> The prestige enjoyed by the notion of freedom of choice has been exploited to great advantage by advocates of what the media has taken to calling "abortion rights." Many Catholics—including a large majority of nationally prominent Catholic politicians and a significant number of notable Catholic theologians—now say that respect for freedom of choice requires Catholics to refrain from acting on their conscientious opposition to abortion in the public forum. In my judgment, this position is philosophically and morally untenable. A choice to give someone else the choice as to whether an innocent third party shall live or die is a choice that no one concerned for basic human rights should be willing to make. Moreover, a proper understanding of the moral significance of human choosing makes it plain that such a choice is one that no Catholic whose conscience is properly formed regarding the injustice of abortion can afford to make.[7]

A vote for this type of candidate guarantees the continued murder of innocent humans. He or she won't lift a finger to help the 1.3 million neighbors who are dying every year. To this person, abortion is not morally wrong before God—it is only *privately* wrong.

There is no such thing as *private* sin. Sin affects all of those around us. Candidates who are "personally against abortion" are wolves in sheep's clothing. God will hold both that candidate *and the voter* accountable.

Rape and Incest

A 1996 Gallup Poll revealed that 77 percent of Americans believe that abortion should be legal for rape and incest.[8] Following such unspeakable trauma, who could imagine having to deal with the unwanted pregnancy?

The first aspect we must consider is the extreme rarity of

this problem. There is only a 1 to 5 percent chance that a rape will result in a pregnancy.[9] Abortions for alleged rape pregnancies account for only 1 to 5 percent of all abortions.[10, 11] The media has exploited this emotional nightmare to justify the murders of millions of humans.

Many people are now aware that the public was deceived in the case of *Roe v. Wade.* Norma McCorvey (Roe) had been publicized as a rape victim. She now confesses that it was a fraud. Her attorneys convinced her to lie for the "good of women."[12] A danger of such a rape exception is that anyone can claim to be raped.

But what about those rare cases when women have suffered this frightening experience and do become pregnant? Do they feel better after an abortion? A child born of such a rape says, "No."

> Women pregnant by assault say their abortion was not the "easy" answer they were led to believe; in fact, some have described it as "medical rape." The feelings of guilt, violation, anger and depression caused by the original assault were compounded by their guilt feelings about the abortion.[13]

A woman who chooses to keep her child can indeed love her baby. That baby is not "the rapist's child"—it is her own child. This child is at no higher risk for antisocial or criminal behavior. Children born from incest are not destined to be deformed. These unborn children have millions of parents waiting to adopt them. There is no compelling reason to kill an innocent human as a result of rape or incest.

Carol Everett, a Texas abortion clinic operator, confesses that she purposefully exploited such myths. She even advertised free abortions for rape. But she admits in her book, *The Scarlet Lady: Confessions of a Successful Abortionist*, "We never did one free abortion on a rape victim."[14]

Donald M. Lake, associate professor of theology at Wheaton College stated:

> In my judgment, neither rape nor anticipated physical or neurological deformity are legitimate reasons [sic] for an abortion.[15]

You cannot justify killing *any* innocent person when you see the unborn human as a complete person in the eyes of natural law and God. To continue to exploit these exceptions of exceedingly rare cases sabotages our ability to save millions of our unborn neighbors.

A nice, young, Christian woman I know is strongly pro-life. But one evening she went to a party where she was given an intoxicating drink without her knowledge. While intoxicated, she had intercourse with an acquaintance and became pregnant. Due to her natural feelings of injustice over the situation, she chose to have an abortion. Was this the just thing to do? I don't think so.

Mary Meehan, pro-life author of "Facing the Hard Cases," explains the thinking process:

> Honesty requires us to say that it is unjust that a woman must carry to term a child who is conceived in rape, but it is a far greater injustice to kill the child. This is a rare situation in which injustice cannot be avoided; the best that can be done is to reduce it. The first injustice lasts for nine months of a life that can be relieved, both psychologically and financially. The second injustice ends a life, and there is no remedy for that.[16]

Tinting the Camel's Nose

Professor Charles Rice of Notre Dame Law School makes this strong statement: "To gain its objective, the pro-life movement must demand that the law fulfill, without exception, its duty to protect innocent life." Why does he say this?

Some women in these tough situations have allowed the child to live. They are pleased with that decision. Others who allowed that child to be murdered continue to grieve over their decision.

The question comes down to this: Is it *ever* justifiable to kill an innocent human? Is it *ever* justifiable to kill a human that is mentally retarded, has a disability, is unwanted, or has the wrong parent? The moment we answer "yes" to any of these situations we are well down the road to genocide. The killing of *any* innocent human life endangers us all.

A person could still be pro-life and believe it's okay to kill humans conceived by rape and incest. However, that stand undermines the very foundation of human responsibility in society; and, the right to life endowed by our Creator. This is the proverbial "camel's nose under the tent." The logic is tinted.

To be consistent, a person should be against abortion in cases of rape and incest. Unquestionably, the emotional trauma of such an event is devastating. Some Christians have been consistent in helping these victims of rape and incest. These women need our love, emotional *and financial* support. Adoption can help. That's one way we can help keep the innocent victim from becoming a victimizer herself.

Conclusions

It is *not always* sin to vote for a pro-choice candidate. If there is *no* pro-life candidate in the race, or a weak pro-life candidate, voting principles should maximize the greatest good of saving as many human lives as possible.

A pro-life candidate understands God's value of human life in natural law. A mother's life is always protected. Using words like "health" and "personally opposed" should raise red flags of deceitful politics.

Rape and incest are frightening emotional issues but we must remember that an innocent human person should not be killed. Any exception may leave the floodgates of continuing murder wide open—1.3 million babies per year. With these concepts in mind, it is relatively easy to prioritize candidates by their stand for life. The candidate who most closely matches God's absolute standard to preserve innocent human life should receive our vote. That candidate is then responsible to God for his or her actions.

Notes

1. Personal correspondence with the author, 12 October 1999.

2. Solzhenitsyn, A.I., *The Oak and the Calf,* 1975, *The Trinity Forum,* 1992, "The most terrible danger of all is that you may do violence to your conscience."

3. Flake, N., "New Christian Coalition chapter in County," *Conroe Courier* (21 November 1999): 1A.

4. Center for Disease Control, *AP/NY Times* (Atlanta, GA: 27 January 1995).

5. Thompson, D., "Woman's sacrifice captures nation's heart," *Springfield News* (18 February 1995): 1.

6. *Doe v. Bolton*, 410 U.S. 179 (1973).

7. George, R., *Conscience and the Public Person*, 217-233.

8. Gallup Poll, *Public Opinion 1996* (Scholarly Resources, 1997), 113.

9. Holmes, M.M., et. al., "Rape Related Pregnancies: Estimates and Descriptive Characteristics from a National Sample of Women," *American Journal of Obstetrics and Gynecology*, 175 (August 1996).

10. Ibid., 320. This is an estimated 32,101 rape pregnancies to 1.4 million abortions.

11. Evrard, J., and Gold, E., "Epidemiology and Management of Sexual Assault Victims," *OB & GYN*, vol. 53, no. 3 (March 1979): 381-387.

12. McCorvey, N., *Won By Love* (Nashville, TN: Thomas Nelson Publishers, 1997), 241. Norma is now a Christian and speaks for the Pro-life position. We were privileged to have her speak at our Right to Life conference in Oregon on 1 April 2000.

13. Makimaa, J., and Kathy Hoffmaster, *The Hard Cases of Abortion* (Washington, DC: Family Research Council, 2000), 38.

14. Everett, C., with Jack Shaw, *The Scarlet Lady: Confession of a Successful Abortionist* (Wolgemuth and Hyatt Publishers, 1991), 134-135.

15. Hoffmeister, J.K., *Abortion: A Christian Understanding and Response* (Grand Rapids, MI: Baker Book House, 1987), 94-95.

16. Meehan, M., "Facing the Hard Cases," *Human Life Review 4*, no. 3 (September 1983): 19.

Voting the Tougher Choices

If we don't vote, won't we lessen our risk of proliferating evil? Jesus also answers this question in the parable of the Good Samaritan.

To Vote or Not To Vote?

The religious leaders in the parable did not harm the dying man. But Jesus intimated that it was not good enough to "do no harm." This would be like a doctor who never treats anyone; he lessens the risk of doing harm.

We are to help our dying neighbor, whether or not we caused the problem. Not to vote is to not help. Not to vote is to not love our neighbor. Not to vote is sin.

We may be disillusioned with politicians; still we have an obligation to help our unborn, dying neighbor. We are called to act, whether or not we think we can win. A surgeon cannot successfully restore perfect health or function in every operation. But we do our best every time.

Since Jesus' parable doesn't have an ending, we don't know if the man survived or died. If he died, did the Samaritan waste his time and money? Of course not. The ending doesn't change the priority. Jesus' message is this: we are to show love for our neighbor through our actions, regardless of the outcome.

Practical Versus Principle Voting

Should we vote for a third-party candidate with a perfect pro-life view, or a major Party candidate with a mediocre pro-life view?

Christians may disagree, and the truth is, there is no perfect answer. Personally, I would like to see a Biblical Party candidate with one *priority* issue on the campaign platform to save innocent human life. This party would stand up for the lives of those killed by abortion murder, euthanasia murder, physician assisted suicide murder, and infanticide.

There should be enough Christians in America with a biblical worldview to vote to protect all innocent human life. If all those who claim to believe that "Jesus is the Christ who died for their sins" followed His command to love our neighbor as the priority, we could win a third-party race.

Money and voting are usually the last two rooms to be opened to the Lordship of Christ, right behind sex. Since that's true, believers in Jesus Christ must experience a revival in which we awaken to God's holiness and His requirements. This is the only way we can make the needed impact in the voting process.

People *are* becoming more dissatisfied. Perhaps within the next few years, a viable third-party may emerge with a strong social and moral platform—more consistent with the Scriptures. If such a party does emerge, let's support it. For now, put personal morality in society above the economy in order to save as many lives as possible.

In the immediate future, we Christians should attempt to place the strongest pro-life candidate in office. Abraham Lincoln followed a similar pattern in his moral struggle against slavery.

Lincoln's Position

Abraham Lincoln was both principled and pragmatic. He was uncompromising in his insistence that slavery violated natural law. But he was wise enough to know this: Moral injustice would never be made right until public opinion was changed.

One of Lincoln's generals ordered the emancipation of slaves in three southern states the year after Lincoln took office. The President, as chief commander, countermanded it. Yet one month after taking office he had said, "On the territorial question, I am inflexible. . . . You think slavery is right and ought to be extended; we think it is wrong and ought to be restricted."[1]

His stated goal was to

> arrest the further spread of it, and place it where the public mind shall rest in the belief that it is in course of ultimate extinction. . . . Lincoln knew that in the final analysis durable judicial rulings on major issues must be rooted in the soil of American opinion. "Public sentiment," he said, "is everything" in this country.[2]

History proved him correct. The Civil War triumphed over the Dred Scott decision within ten years. But state-imposed racial segregation lasted fifty-eight years before *Brown v. Education* overturned it. We continue to battle against racism because we continue to struggle against public opinion.

How Pro-Life Must We Vote?

What if one candidate supported total abolition of abortion while another candidate made exceptions for rape and incest. Who would win? The latter candidate. That's because 77 percent of Americans think abortion should be allowed for rape and incest.[3]

Until Americans are educated and opinion changed, voting for candidates who are ahead of the public will result in defeat. Push for legislation that coincides with what is morally right, and is also supported by the majority of Americans. With this strategy, we will ultimately win life and liberty for the unborn.

How can we say that not voting to save as many lives as possible is sin, then turn around and say to vote strategically? This is the foundation of Lincoln's position. In terms of the sanctity of human life, this means the uncompromising fight for eventual complete emancipation of the unborn from the death grip of abortion—while presently pressing to persuade the American public step by step with education.

Since the majority of women already believe that abortion is wrong except for cases of rape and incest, we should push legislation based on that moral stand. After that victory, we can educate the public on the horror of killing a child from the wrong parent, and the added suffering of the mother who would abort it.

Partial Birth Abortions

This procedure should be the number one priority for education and legislation. We can visualize the delivering of the entire baby outside of the mother's body except for the head—just like a breech delivery. But instead of delivering the head, the scissors are rammed into the skull and the brains sucked out. Highlighting this barbaric procedure can win the debate.

The American Medical Association has publicly stated that this procedure is *never* needed to save the life of the mother. Any person who can support this procedure as "necessary" can only mean necessary for financial or political gain.

The majority of Americans wanted partial birth abortions banned, and Congress twice passed legislation to outlaw it. Unfortunately, the President vetoed it twice.

How does the President who wants abortion to be "safe, legal, and rare" justify such an act? How can he force other countries to accept mass abortion by holding them as financial hostages? Jesus used one word for such a person—"hypocrite."

Pro-choice people are hypocritical as well, because they don't really want abortion to be rare—at least their actions betray this hypocrisy. But many pro-life people are *also* hypocritical, because they continue to vote for pro-choice candidates. How can you believe the fetus to be a complete person made in the image of God, yet vote to allow it to be killed? Pro-choice and pro-life supporters *both* need a reality check.

Twenty-seven states have passed bans on the torture of the nearly born—partial birth abortions.[4] For Wisconsin and Illinois, this resulted in a judicial stay of enforcement. It is scheduled to come before the Supreme Court this year. The November 2000 Presidential election is even more critical since the next President may appoint as many as three Supreme Court Justices. This could significantly alter the balance of power.

The Candidates Lagging and Leading

A particular candidate running for the 2000 Republican nomination had historically been pro-life. However, when asked if overturning *Roe v. Wade* would be a good idea, this man once replied, "No." He doesn't favor ending abortion legislatively in the short term or long term since there is a "need" for it.[5]

When asked about his position on abortion, this candidate assaulted "otherwise intelligent people who say that that's the only issue that will determine their vote."[6] This may be one more case of a politician swerving from what's morally right to gain advantage in an election. Let's hope not.

There is a long list of prior pro-life supporters who have eventually become militantly pro-choice to kill humans and harm women. It includes Edward Kennedy, Jesse Jackson, Al Gore, and Bill Clinton. The political advantage becomes obvious when we see a national Party refusing to allow a liberal governor—on every issue except abortion—speak at his own Democratic national convention.[7]

In contrast, there is a presidential candidate who has precisely followed Lincoln's strategy. As a governor, he has passed more life-saving legislation in his state (nine bills) than any other governor. This candidate declared, "I support a constitutional amendment with the exceptions of life, rape, and incest."[8]

The National Abortion Rights Action League has even run television ads against him.[9] NARAL's President, Kate Michelman, called him the most "anti-choice" governor in America.[10] Now, here is an interesting way to determine whom you can trust—listen to the opposition. NARAL endorsed Vice-President Al Gore for the 2000 presidential election. "In accepting the endorsement, Mr. Gore vowed, 'As President, with your help, I will make sure that the right to choose is never threatened, never weakened and never taken away.' " "I've always supported *Roe v. Wade*." [11] Those are radical statements considering we are now legally killing viable human persons by partial birth abortions (brain-sucking.)

Guidelines to Effective Voting

Voters' guides outline various positions—especially candidates' voting records on saving unborn children. A guide from NARAL or *Planned Parenthood* will tell us whom to avoid. A guide from a *Right to Life* organization will help educate us on who supports life.

A lot of careful work goes into a decision to support a candidate by a *Right to Life* organization. If you cannot take the time to educate yourself through personal attention to the candidates, at least read the voter's guides. An endorsement by *Right to Life* for a particular candidate doesn't guarantee that he or she will be everything we want, but it's a good place to start.

If there are two candidates—one pro-choice and one pro-life, the decision should be for the pro-life candidate. If both candidates are pro-choice, is there one who opposes partial birth abortions?

The following positions would then be scrutinized:

Does he or she support parental notification of teenage abortions? Licensing of abortion clinics? Denying tax-exempt status to not-for-profit organizations that perform, refer for, or assist in abortions, such as *Planned Parenthood?* Prohibiting family planning funding to organizations that offer abortion procedures?

If these aren't available, the candidate who opposes euthanasia should be chosen. If two pro-life candidates are in a primary, the strongest pro-life candidate should be chosen. If both are strong, other issues should be considered.

If two pro-life candidates are in a general election, and one is a major party and one is a third-party candidate, it's wise to vote for the major party candidate. To split the vote among pro-life candidates usually results in *both* of them losing.[12] I recommend this majority vote even if the majority candidate is not quite as strong in the pro-life position as a third-party candidate.

The candidate's position must be somewhat close to the public's position to win. Once in office, the candidate's supporters can work to educate and persuade from a respected platform.

Conclusions

When we vote, we help save our neighbor; when we fail to vote, we sin. A pro-choice vote is sinful if there is a pro-life candidate in the race. We must make the banning of partial birth abortions a priority, and enact whatever constructive legislation we can to emancipate unborn Americans. Meanwhile, we must be educating the public in fetology and the importance of natural law.

Pro-choice people need to begin acting upon their stated positions to make abortion safe, legal, and rare. Pro-life people need to begin acting upon their position that abortion kills our neighbors.

Candidates with proven track records of protecting the unborn should receive our votes. Beware of candidates who switch their view on sanctity of life issues. Voters' guides from *Right to Life* will help us in determining the candidates most likely to deliver the unborn from mass death.[13]

Notes

1. McKenna, G., "On Abortion: A Lincolnian Position," *Atlantic Monthly* (September 1995), 61.

2. Ibid., 60.

3. The Gallup Organization, the Gallup Poll: Public Opinion 1996 (Scholarly Resources, Inc., 1997), 113.

4. Andrusko, D., "Justice Stevens Stays Enforcement of Partial Birth Abortion Laws," *National Right to Life News* (December 1999): 5.

5. Andrusko, D., "It's Only Business," *National Right to Life News* (December 1999): 28, concerning Senator John McCain.

6. Ibid., 2.

7. McKenna, G., "On Abortion: A Lincolnian Position," *Atlantic Monthly* (September 1995), 61, concerning Governor Robert Casey of Pennsylvania in 1992.

8. Bush, George W., "Interview with Tim Russert" on *NBC's Meet the Press* (21 November 1999).

9. "NARAL Attacks Bush Again," *National Right to Life News* (December 1999): 25. The insert quotes the New Hampshire television ad during the Republican presidential candidate debate on 2 December 1999.

10. Tobias, C., "What Pro-lifers Could Learn from King Solomon," *National Right to Life News* (January 2000): 6.

11. Cain, A., and combined dispatches, "Multiple choice? Bradley presses Gore on abortion record," *The Washington Times, National Weekly Edition* (21-27 February 2000): 26.

12. Right to Life may be contacted on the web at http://nrlc.org/news/index.html.

15.

Political Objections

There are sincere Christians who love God and yet have objections to this position of spiritual voting. These objections fall into three categories—political/legal, theological, and personal.

Since I once thought the way that they now think, I know how vital it is to challenge these ways of thinking. One day we'll stand before Holy God to give an account of what we have done here on earth. At that time, all of our objections will be overruled. May He continue to open our eyes to His truth. As St. Augustine cried, "Let truth, the light of my heart, speak to me and not my own darkness!"[1]

Argument 1:
Voting should not depend upon only one issue.

Draw a line to form two columns. Place 1.3 million human beings killed on one side and then number 1 through 5 on the other side. List the other items such as taxes, women's rights, education, social security, or any other combination of issues. Which ones outweigh the need to save 1.3 million humans every year?

This is not one issue voting. This is priority voting—God's priority. This is "Seek ye first the Kingdom of God and His righteousness" voting. To label sanctity of life issues as single issue voting is a straw man argument. Voting pro-life is *priority* voting.

Let's suppose that saving 1.3 million pregnant women were placed against saving 1.3 million newborn humans. In that case, we should choose the pregnant women because this choice would rescue twice the number of humans from death. In this scenario, abortion would not be the one issue on which the vote was decided.

The principle is to vote in accordance with God's priority of righteousness: We are to save as many lives as possible. Keep in mind that God's righteousness is not merely a theological position in Christ. It is a *practical* righteousness to be lived out in us day by day.

Argument 2:
We always lose.

Some have asked if we really do any good by voting pro-life. These people say we always lose. Besides, the issue only comes up for a vote once in a while.

I would remind these people that both the U.S. House and Senate voted and twice passed a ban on sucking the brains out of babies who would have lived (*partial birth abortion* is a euphemism). Congress nearly overrode a veto by President Clinton. The sad fact is that the babies—God's priority—lost by only three votes. One vote was by our own Senator from Oregon, Ron Wyden, a vocal women-have-the-right-to-kill-their-babies-supporter for whom many *Christians* voted.

Many Christians also voted for President Clinton, who was strongly and unashamedly pro-choice. This president has been personally responsible for continuing the horrible sin and crime of partial birth abortions. He has personally authorized thousands of killings per year—against the wishes of the Congress and the majority of the American people. Pray for him.

President Clinton has also pushed abortion in foreign countries by withholding financial aid until abortions are encouraged. There are now forty-six million abortions in the world each year.[2] How long will it take for us Christians to see that this authorization to murder (in order to obtain other goals) is sin?

A second answer to the objection that we always lose can be found once again in the Good Samaritan. Did the man survive from the care given by the Good Samaritan? Did he die despite this care because his wounds and beatings were so severe?

The Good Samaritan was not good because the man lived or died—*the outcome was irrelevant*. The Good Samaritan changed his priorities to attempt to save the life of a fellow human being. If we love our neighbor as Jesus commanded, we will keep trying to save human lives regardless of the outcome.

Why do we always lose? Because *Christians* are not voting, and not voting God's priority.

Argument 3:
The Church is not a political body.

True. The *reductio ad absurdum* argument in Chapter 7 proved the fallacy of this reasoning. The Church is not a political body, a bank, a financial institution, or a symphony orchestra.

Yes, the Church should not spend the majority of time and energy on anything that is more political than moral. I agree that the purpose of the four gospels was not to give Jesus' political views. But let's take a close look.

In claiming political noninvolvement, Christians point to the fact that Jesus did not take the political headship of Israel when the crowds offered it to Him. A careful student of the Scriptures should not be surprised that Jesus did not accept a political position at the first advent.

The assumption is that Jesus did not *want* a political position. This could not be further from the truth! The reason He was not willing to accept the position *at that time* was that the crowds were solely interested in a political deliverer from Roman oppression. They were not interested in spiritual salvation.

Jesus' words to Pilate in John 18:36 are also misunderstood. Jesus said His kingdom was not "of this world." He also said that He, Himself, was not "of this world" (John 8:23). Does that mean that He was not physically present on the earth? His point was heavenly origin and essence. We cannot use this passage to say that He and his kingdom will not come physically to the earth.

Jesus *did* want Israel to accept Him as their King, both spiritually and politically (Matt. 23:37-39). The prophet Isaiah proclaims "the government will rest upon His shoulders. . . . There will be no end to the increase of His government or of peace" (Isa. 9:6). Let us not forget that He *will* succeed at the ultimate political coup at His return. Jesus *will be* the political ruler of the entire world and universe. His goals are not merely spiritual. Jesus' goals *are political* in the sense of societal conformity to His law.

It takes very little persuasiveness to teach that voting for pro-choice (to kill humans and harm women) candidates is sin. That's no harder than teaching that voting for a candidate who wants to legalize infant murder would be sin. This does not need to become a litmus test for spirituality. However, when a moral issue is politicized, does that mean we can no longer teach Christians how to act on it?

Bonhoeffer's Germany

Isn't that exactly what happened in Germany prior to World War II? Both church leaders and Christian laypeople claimed that the shipping of the Jews to the camps was a legal governmental operation. It was political: the church had more important concerns—i.e., to preach the gospel.

What's the difference between our American sanctity of life issues versus the German Christians allowing the killing of Jews? Both were—and are—legal and political. Many believe that the German Christians sinned by omission when they failed to help save human beings. Is that any different from actively voting for the death of humans because we have other priorities? Both were—and are—morally wrong and sin.

Some leaders in the German Church called Dietrich Bonhoeffer a misguided political activist. After the Holocaust, he was embraced as a Christian martyr. Today, the skewed thinking of many Christians may again label him a misguided activist.

Political Paranoia

Satan has won a major victory in America to further his kingdom of darkness. His strategic battle plan has been simple. When an entrenched sin is under attack by God's kingdom, simply change sin's uniform to a *political* issue. That way, Christians will not recognize it as sin. They won't touch it, much less fight it. There is an extreme fear of politicizing the Church.

Suppose voting for a candidate could never be sin. Then suppose that the Supreme Court ruled that it was legal to kill

Christian leaders. That is exactly what happened in abortion and slavery. Of course, we personally would not kill Christian leaders. But, if someone else thought it was necessary to prevent the spread of this harmful religion, then they'd have that legal right to choose.

What if a candidate was on the ballot who was known to consistently vote to allow the killing of Christian leaders? We wouldn't vote for him for the *purpose* of killing Christian leaders. Suppose we voted for him because of his stand on other important issues. Then we'd be willing to authorize the death of 1.5 million Christian leaders every year to get what we want.

We would then consider killing Christians to be a *political* issue. So, of course we wouldn't have the right to tell people that voting for a candidate who backs the killing of Christian leaders is a sin. It might be seriously wrong, but not a sin.

John the Baptist—or the Politician?

Did John the Baptist politicize the gospel of Jesus when he spoke out against the sin of Herod taking his brother's wife? King Herod was not a synagogue-going Jew. In fact, he was not even respected as a Jew—he was only partly Jewish.

Herod's sin did not affect the Jewish community directly. It was not the primary issue of John's message to the Jews about Jesus. Yet, John was willing to risk his life to expose the sin of this "political" moral issue. He was killed for it.[3]

When the moral and political collide—God's Church *should stand strong* to preach against the evil of immorality! To do anything less is to approve of their evil deeds by default.

John the Baptist believed that taking a strong moral stand against political sin was worth the risk of dying. John the Baptist and Dietrich Bonhoeffer both showed us the correct response to the politics of sin. Germany's sincere but pragmatic church leaders showed us the wrong response. What will be our response?

Abraham Lincoln

President Abraham Lincoln was all too familiar with this deceptive objection about bringing politics into religion. In 1860,

the churches in America had the exact same response to slavery:
It's political. To Judge Douglas, Lincoln responded piercingly:

> If you examine the arguments that are made on it, you will
> find that every one carefully excludes the idea that there is
> anything wrong in slavery. Perhaps the Democrat who says
> he is as much opposed to slavery as I am, will tell me that
> I am wrong about this. I wish him to examine his own
> course in regard to this matter a moment, and then see if
> his opinion will not be changed a little. You say it is wrong;
> but don't you constantly object to anybody else saying so?
> Do you not constantly argue that this is not the *right place*
> to oppose it? You say it must not be opposed in the Free
> States, because slavery is not here; it must not be opposed
> in the Slave States, because it is there; it must not be
> opposed in politics, because that will make a fuss; *it must
> not be opposed in the pulpit, because it is not religion*. [Loud
> cheers.] Then where is the place to oppose it? *There is no
> suitable place to oppose it*. There is no plan in the country to
> oppose this evil overspreading the continent, which you
> say yourself is coming. Frank Blair and Gratz Brown tried
> to get up a system of gradual emancipation in Missouri,
> had an election in August, and got beat, and you, Mr.
> Democrat, threw up your hat, and hallooed "Hurrah for
> Democracy." [Enthusiastic cheers.][4] (emphasis added)

As wrong as American slavery was, it cannot compare to
the millions of humans dying every year from abortion murder.
Why do they die? Because, as Mr. Lincoln said, *neither church
leaders nor politicians will do* anything to let us stop the wrong.

It's not enough to say so privately; we must see abortion
killing as *wrong enough to act*—not "buy in" to the fallacy that
it's wrong to bring religion into politics.

What we Americans need today is a courageous, moral
leader such as President Lincoln to chastise us again!

Argument 4:
Voting only for Pro-life candidates would be political because all Pro-life candidates are Republicans.

Most pro-life candidates are Republicans. However, there
are Democratic candidates who vote pro-life.

Congressman Alan Mollohan, Democrat of West Virginia, has been a champion of pro-life efforts since 1983, when he joined the House of Representatives. He received the Thomas Jefferson Pursuit of Life Award, sponsored by nine pro-life organizations: National Right to Life, Catholic Alliance, Christian Coalition, Concerned Women for America, Family Research Council, Feminists for Life, Justice Fellowship, National Coalition of Pro-Life Democrats, Religious Freedom Coalition, and Traditional Values Coalition.[5]

Most people are not aware of a National Coalition of Pro-Life Democrats. Here's a quote from a Democrats for Life web-site: "A 1999 Gallup survey showed that nearly three out of four adults in America would outlaw more than 90 percent of abortions. Isn't it time that the Democratic Party's platform reflected the view of the people?"[6]

In contrast, there *are* Republican candidates who are in favor of the right to kill humans and harm women. Christine Todd-Whitman, Governor of New Jersey, has been a strong Republican voice for pro-choice. Therefore, this is not a question of Party affiliation or preference.

George Barna's research in 1999 indicated that 86 percent of Democrats, 93 percent of Republicans, and 83 percent of Independents consider themselves to be Christians.[7] Neither Christianity nor the morality of natural law is a political party controversy. In all parties, all people, especially those who call themselves Christians, should understand and act upon the priority of human life.

Priority Voting

What are we as Christians willing to suffer in order to facilitate God's priority of life? Higher taxes, less freedom of choice, more work for *us* to educate our children, less retirement security, etc.?

Political parties are irrelevant to the discussion. All other party platforms and issues are secondary. The truth has become evident that neither Democrats, nor Republicans, nor Libertarians, nor Reform Party politicians, have been seriously committed to God's priority of life. Political Party preference is politics. Pro-life priority is biblical Christianity.

A Christian should *never* vote along party lines. Every candidate should be evaluated individually as to his or her stand on life issues such as abortion. To the follower of Jesus Christ, all other issues must be secondary.

Wouldn't it be nice if that helpful "Christian Voters Guide" would leave off Party affiliations? Then we could get to God's will in human society: who favors the preservation of innocent human life? The liberty of life is our primary politic.

Conclusions

Pro-life voting is not the only issue—it is the *priority* issue. We often lose because confused Christians are either not voting, or voting against God. The Church *can* teach about voting because it directly affects sin and salvation. The Church *can* teach that it is a sin to vote for the continuation of mass murder of people made by God in His image. This is the position that the Church should *return* to teaching.

It is *not* political to stand with candidates who uphold God's righteous standards. We do *not* stand by Parties or platforms. We stand by individual candidates who are committed to God's priority of life—made in His image.

If we do not speak out about sin now, our freedom to obey Christ without suffering may be short-lived. John the Baptist, Abraham Lincoln, and Dietrich Bonhoeffer have shown us the way.

Notes

1. St. Augustine of Hippo, *The Confessions of St. Augustine* (New York: Mentor-Omega Books), 290.

2. Gardiner, B., "Twenty-two percent of pregnancies end in abortion, data show," *The Oregonian* (22 January 2000): A10.

3. Matthew 14:1-13.

4. Lincoln, A., *Lincoln-Douglas Debates*, Sixth Debate, Quincy, 13 October 1858; accessed 11 February 2000; available from http://www.umsl.edu/~virtualstl/dred_scott_case/texts/deb6.htm.

5. Andrusko, D., Ed., "Congressman Mollohan, Pro-life Democrat, Receives 'Pursuit of Life' Award," *National Right to Life News* (December 1999): 15.

6. Democrats for Life of America, Inc., accessed 11 February 2000; available from http://www.democratsforlife.org/brochure.html.

7. "Politics," Barna Research Online, accessed 20 February 2000; available from http://www.barna.org/cgi-bin/PageCategory.asp?categoryID=31. Updated 17 February 2000.

16.

Theological Objections

Most of us have positions of responsibility with children, employees, or parishioners. It is difficult to see people whom we love do things that harm themselves and others.

Many different Christian leaders have defended their lack of action on abortion voting through the following arguments. I love them and continue to pray for them, that God will open their eyes to *His* priorities. I pray that God will answer all of their theological "objections."

Argument 1:
Abortion is not a priority because Jesus
does not mention it, even though infanticide
occurred during Jesus' time on Earth.

I agree that the issue of abortion is not mentioned in the New Testament, and that infanticide was occurring during Jesus' time on earth—in Greece, for example. As far as we know, it was not occurring in Israel when Jesus was an adult.

Jesus did not address infanticide or abortion to our knowledge. Jesus did not address homosexuality, either. Does this mean that it is not sin or not important? In fact, neither Jesus nor the New Testament mentions euthanasia, bestiality, sacrificing children to the idols through fire, pornography, or even the tithing/stewardship giving of 10 percent for that matter. The only source for our knowledge that abortion itself is sin is the Old Testament—outside of the recorded words of Jesus.

Are God's principles of *moral* standards in the Old Testament nullified because they are not repeated in the New Testament? Do we as the Church really want to go down that road? Are the only important words in the Bible those few words recorded about what Jesus said or did in the four gospels?

God punished Israel and Judah severely for the infanticide that occurred in the Old Testament. In 2 Chronicles 33:6 and 9, the sin of King Manasseh of Judah is recorded: ". . . and he caused his children to pass through the fire in the valley of Hinnom . . . so Manasseh made Judah and the inhabitants of Jerusalem to err and to do worse than the nations whom the Lord had destroyed before the children of Israel."

Other examples of God's judgment on infanticide by child sacrifice are recorded by the prophet in Ezekiel 23:39: "for when they had slain their children to their idols." Was Jesus not familiar with these? Did He not realize that God was furious over this infanticide? Was Jesus' opinion different from God the Father's opinion? I think not. We may not have Jesus' thoughts on infanticide because it was not a problem in Israel when he was on earth. To argue from Jesus' silence on abortion in this case is an elementary (theo)logical error. Infanticide was, and still is, a priority for God—because preserving innocent human life is God's priority.

Argument 2:
The Bible does not call voting a sin;
therefore, we should not try to make it a sin.

The Bible does not mention voting. Therefore, the Bible cannot state that voting is a sin. The Bible does not mention pornography—therefore, is pornography not a sin?

The foundational question in this argument is—are all possible sins covered in the Bible? Could a list of *all* possible specific sins be found from reading the Bible?

Three areas of latitude exist in this realm of sin—law, principle, and freedom. There are those who would say that we can only call sin what the Bible specifically calls sin. These specific laws are all we need to know and we may not add to them. These laws about sin are the dogma of the Church.

However, this view leaves out the principles in the Bible. There are sins recognized by the collective wisdom of the Church through the ages. Although not specifically stated to be sin, the Church has recognized these acts as sin. Suicide would be an example, since there is no prohibition against killing one's self— only murder of *another* person.

The third and greatest latitude is freedom of opinion. These are actions or omissions or attitudes that are not addressed in the Bible either specifically or by principle. These cannot be called sins, but should be a matter of choice for the individual Christian and the individual church.

Principles

When we claim that only those sins specifically mentioned in the Bible are sins, we ignore the principles. Jesus taught *principles* more than He taught specific sins. In fact, He took the specific sins taught in the Jewish Bible and expanded on them as principles. "You have heard that it has been said, . . . but I say unto you . . ." (Matt. 5:21, 27, 33, 38, 43).

Jesus expanded the specific sin of murder to include being angry with a brother without cause, and calling another person worthless (a fool). He expanded the specific sin of physical adultery to include the principles of lust of the heart and divorce. He expanded the command to love your neighbor to include your enemy as your neighbor. Jesus also gave the story of the Good Samaritan to demonstrate that loving our neighbor requires action and sacrifice to help those in need (even if that neighbor is antagonistic toward us.) If we do not obey that commandment—loving our neighbors as ourselves—we sin.

Do we take this to mean that we only need to love our neighbor if we find him beaten and robbed, and left to die on the side of the road? What if our dying neighbor is not on the side of the road, but still in the car?

Would it be sin to go around on the other side of the road without helping that dying person live? Jesus did not call it sin. The Bible never says it is sin. How could we call it a sin? Because it was not loving my neighbor, it violates His principle.

Jesus taught *principles of sin*—not merely specific sins.

Principle Applied

Jesus said that loving my neighbor who is dying requires changing my priorities, and acting to save that person from death. The unborn are the victims of abortion violence resulting in death unless we have compassion. If we have mercy on the dying and act to save their lives, we will have loved our neighbor.

This principle of caring for those who cannot help themselves is championed in Proverbs 31:8-9. "Open your mouth for those who cannot speak—for the cause of all those who are appointed to death. Open your mouth, judge righteously, and plead the cause of the poor and needy."

The unborn in the womb certainly fit this description. We are commanded to protect the defenseless ones who are condemned to die. Remember James, who viewed the love of neighbor similarly? "Pure religion and undefiled before God and the Father is this: to visit the widow and the orphan in their afflictions" (James 1: 27).

Voting Principle

A person claims that abortion is wrong. That person will pray or pronounce a blessing for the unborn child and perhaps speak out against abortion. That person may even help in clinics for abortion alternatives.

However, when it comes time to help stop the mass murder of these neighbors, that same person has other priorities. The priority resides somewhere else rather than to try to stop the mass murder of these neighbors by voting for a pro-life candidate. One of the most important actions necessary for life itself is undone. Perhaps James' response would be the same: that faith is dead.

I am acquainted with a Christian woman who strongly supports Crisis Pregnancy Centers. She helps to raise money and walks in the marathon. After working together on a project, I was quite surprised to learn that she will often vote for a pro-choice candidate. I congratulated her for helping to save a few children per year; however, I then had to ask my friend a tough question. "Why do you save a few children each year, but then vote to allow 1.3 million to die every year?"

There is no question that this woman is a Christian. However, her faith alone will not help save unborn children. In this one particular issue of life, her faith is dead—useless—it *is not* caring for the lives of those in need.[1] She needs to *change* her priorities to align them with Jesus' priorities. This is necessary in order for her to be changed into the image of Christ in His Holiness (sanctified) here on earth. This is God's *priority* principle.

Principles in the New Testament

The apostle Paul emphasizes the principle as the foundation in Romans 13:8-10.

> Do not owe anything to anybody except to love one another. The person who loves another has fulfilled the law; because, all of these—Thou shalt not commit adultery, thou shalt not murder, thou shalt not steal, thou shalt not bear false witness, thou shalt not covet—and if there is any other commandment, it can be summarized in this saying: Thou shalt love thy neighbor as thyself. Love does not work harm to a neighbor.

James also emphasizes principle in chapter four, speaking about planning for the future.[2]

Loving our neighbor is the foundational commandment among people in society. To *not* love our neighbor is a foundational sin. To vote for any other priority instead of to save our neighbor's life is *not* loving our neighbor. To vote for any other priority is to allow our neighbor to die from violent abortion murder. Voting pro-choice *is* sin.

Today, we Christians have controversial matters of sin similar to the New Testament example of eating of meat sacrificed to idols. Some persons believe that going to movies, dancing, drinking alcohol, gambling, and other such things are sin. These can be harmful, and some may indeed be sin.

But I see a difference between these possible sins and voting pro-choice (to murder babies). It is the same difference that Jesus pointed out to us. *A life of our neighbor is at stake. Certain death results unless we act.* A wrong opinion on the other issues may be harmful. However, all of them combined cannot touch the atrocity of 1.3 million murders each year from a vote that allows abortion to continue.

Yes, it is possible that I am wrong. Voting may be merely a matter of freedom and opinion. But is it worth the risk of being held accountable for aiding in 1.3 million murders each year?

In Matthew 25:31-46, Jesus declares it a serious offense not to give food, clothing, and hospitality to those in physical need. How much more not to rescue those who are being killed? Is it worth the risk of hearing these words from our Savior at the judgment seat of Christ?

"I told you to love your dying neighbor enough to change your priorities, and to act to save his and her lives; why didn't you?

Why didn't you obey me? You allowed millions to die.

You did not love your neighbor."

Argument 3:
There are other sins and problems that are more serious.

There *are* other sins and problems in America that are serious. One out of every six abortions is requested by and committed upon a woman who describes herself as a "born-again Christian." In our churches, we know women who have had an abortion.

The Church does not yet comprehend the mass murder for which it is partly responsible. In America, Christ's Church is directly responsible for 240,000 abortion murders every year. Yes, *that is* a more serious sin than a vote that continues the abortion massacre.

There are *too many* issues of serious sin for me to discuss. At the top of the list is the lack of regard for God's holiness that Jesus demands from His bride, the Church. It is appalling. As George Barna points out, one cannot tell the difference between the people in the Church and those outside of it.

> The Bible clearly states that true believers should be readily distinguished from nonbelievers by the way they live. Yet, the evidence undeniably suggests that most American Christians today do not live in a way that is quantifiably different from their non-Christian peers . . .[3]

The major reason that this *particular* sin of abortion voting stands out is the effect it has had upon America. In many minds, the value of human life has been reduced to less than the endangered animals. People can be imprisoned for mistreatment of even domesticated animals while we murder our own babies.

Human life is cheap. Abortion murder has opened the floodgates of sin. The inhumanity and violence of people to each other has become epidemic. The foundational truth of the value of a human being made in the image of God has been trampled. Teenagers are killing other teenagers in school shootings.

If we want to reverse this violence, we must regain the priority of saving the lives of our unborn neighbors. From a pragmatic viewpoint, reversing the violence should be enough reason to vote pro-life as the priority.

Changing Behavior Is Important

From a spiritual viewpoint, why spend the effort to bring attention to this sin of voting? The Church is filled with people who already know of sins and yet, continue to commit them. Divorce, adultery, pornography, premarital sex, greed (robbing God by not being good stewards in tithes and offerings), and many more sins are as prevalent in the Church as they are in the world.

What good does it do to point out another? Will it really make any difference in behavior? Perhaps not.

I have asked God this very question in taking the time to write this book. Why should I bother? Who will listen?

However, the mission of the Church is to teach all nations to obey what Christ has commanded. Our job is to teach them to obey *all* of His commands. If they do not obey, it is then between them and God–God will judge. If we do not teach them to obey, God holds us responsible.

In the larger picture, God will probably hold us more responsible for the national sin of abortion murder than for many other sins. We *cannot* change people's *hearts*. But, we can change their *behavior* by enacting law and expecting moral law to be upheld by society.

Martin Luther King, Jr. eloquently, yet succinctly, explained this concept when he was discussing racism: "Morality cannot be legislated, but behavior can be regulated. Judicial decrees may not change the heart, but they can *restrain the heartless.*"[4]

His principle is proven by the paucity of abortions prior to 1973 followed by the horrific holocaust of thirty-eight million abortion murders since that legal change. Although the change of hearts is ideal, the *restraint of immoral behavior is also a priority goal in society*. As a society, we already regulate morality in every law.

We regulate against rape, theft, kidnapping, violence, and many other moral issues. The question is not "should we regulate morality?" Rather, we should be asking: "whose morality will we be legislating?" Is it constitutional, enforceable, and ethical?[5] Restraint by law is especially important in the case of murder. That was God's priority of restraint of sin between persons in society.

Argument 4:
The unborn children are going to go to heaven anyway.

No, I did not make this one up. A well-meaning Christian actually made this statement to my wife. The assumption in this thinking is simple—in the classic sense of the word.

"Since a baby (person) will be going to heaven anyway, it is okay to kill them." That line of reasoning allows all Christians—men, women, boys and girls—to be murdered with impunity. Murder is a sin regardless of the eternal destination of the victim.

This Christian did quickly realize the absurdity of her statement. However, as the Bible declares, "out of the abundance of the heart the mouth speaks." This was just one of many excuses thrown out to defend the fact that she was in sin by her voting practices.

Argument 5:
Since the unborn child does not yet have a soul, it is not a human person who can be murdered.

Consider the many persons in the Old Testament and New Testament whom God called while they were still in the womb of the mother (Chapter 3). Whether or not these persons had a soul within the womb, God was already calling them to serve Him as humans. God was already preparing these humans in the womb.

Father Frank Pavone is the national director of Priests for Life. He makes an excellent argument that the question of when a child receives a soul is a theological question that does not need to be answered in order to protect human life.

> Suppose, for example, that I do not believe that you have a soul. Does that give me the right to kill you? No. It does not. Your life is still protected by the law, despite my beliefs. Does the law that protects your life require me to believe that you have a soul? No. It does not. It doesn't even require that souls exist at all. What it requires is that whatever I believe, I refrain from taking your life. The law protects both the right to believe and the life of the believer.[6]

Legally, a belief that a soul is present in a person does not decide if that person is a human being. Some people believe that animals have souls while others do not—we do not ponder this question when we convict people of animal abuse.

Killing an endangered animal is still punishable regardless of whether a soul exists. Many atheists and agnostics in this country do not believe that people have souls. Killing human beings is murder regardless of whether or not they have souls.

Conclusions

Restraining the murder of innocent humans is a priority—regardless of whether Jesus spoke on the subject. An argument from silence is a poor logical argument.

Jesus and the apostles taught principles more than specifics—there is a good reason. The Bible does not specifically cover every possible sin. However, God has clearly laid out His principles for us—everything that we need to know about living in a way that pleases Him.

Although there *are* many serious sins, our society has witnessed the disastrous effects of our neglect to uphold God's priority of human life. We already legislate morality in areas such as rape and robbery as we attempt to bring our world to a change of heart toward Jesus Christ. We need to legislate God's priority.

Human life is God's priority—it should be ours.

Notes

1. This may confuse some people. How can I say that her faith is dead in this area, yet say that she is a Christian based on other criteria? A theological position does exist that dissolves the tension between faith and works as used by James and Paul. Only a brief summary is possible here. The New Testament Greek word for "save" (sozo) is used to mean: 1) deliverance from physical death, disease, enemies, 2) the temporal wrath of God on earth, 3.) eternal deliverance from the penalty of sin—justification, 4) eternal deliverance from the presence of sin—glorification, and 5) the temporal deliverance from the power of sin over our lives—sanctification. The same word is used for all of these different types of deliverance. Context must determine the meaning. James could easily mean sanctification salvation since he calls them Christians by using "beloved" and "brothers" twenty times. The use of the word *dead* does not mean false. Comparing Romans 6:1-12, Paul tells us that we are dead to sin but sin does keep acting on us. The opposite of dead is not false, but alive—what was dead was once alive. We are dead to sin, the law, and dead with Christ. Therefore, this passage does not specifically say that those persons are not Christians. It is an assumption to say *dead* must refer to an unbeliever. It may mean that the brother is not being saved from the power of sin—sanctification. See Dr. John Hart, "How to Energize Your Faith: Reconsidering the Meaning of James 2:14-16" *Journal of the Grace Evangelical Society* (Spring 1999), 37-66. Dr. John Hart is Professor of Bible at Moody Bible Institute.

2. The context is a person gloating over a business plan that will bring a large profit. James warns the person that he or she does not even know if tomorrow will come. Death may come tonight. James advises the person to say, "if the Lord desires that I live, I will do it." Then James tells us it is sin not to say this to each other when planning. "Therefore, to him that knows he should do good, and yet does not do it, to him it is sin." Does this sin apply only to profit margins? The principle is the key—not the specific. Whenever I presume upon the future without acknowledging God's rule over my very life, it is sin. That is the principle. To limit sin to only what is specifically written as sin is to ignore the principle. This was one of Jesus' indictments against the Pharisees.

The apostle Paul states a similar principle in Romans 14:23. "For whatever is not of faith is sin." The context is a person who is unsure about rules such as eating meat sacrificed to idols. That person is not aware of the freedom in Christ and thinks it may be wrong to eat the meat. He eats it anyway because he wants it. Although eating the meat was not sin, the acting without faith was sin. The context makes it clear that the emphasis is not on eating meat, but on a clear conscience before God by faith. Again, to focus on the specific sin is to ignore the principle. *The principle* is the priority.

3. Barna, G., *The Second Coming of the Church,* 121.

4. King, M.L., Jr., *Strength to Love* (William Collins and World Publishing, 1963), 33.

5. Geisler, N.L., and Frank S. Turek, *Legislating Morality* (Minneapolis, MN: Bethany House Publishers, 1998), 15-54.

6. Pavone, F., "Religious Beliefs, Abortion, and the Law," *Priests for Life,* accessed 15 February 2000; available from http://www.priestsforlife.org/brochures/relbeliefsandlaw.htm.

17.

Personal Objections

We may have priorities and defenses that prevent us from seeing God's truth. The problem may not be a failure to be convinced of the truth. Perhaps we do not *want* to believe the truth. Knowing that might be the case for me, I prayerfully ask myself some questions. Would you do the same?

- What would make it difficult for me to commit myself to stand for God's sanctity of life?
- What fortress or stronghold have I held back from surrender to the Lordship of Jesus Christ?
- What's at risk for me personally?
- What would I have to *change* if I believed that God's Word demanded that I stop sinning by my vote?

Since our minds do not surrender to the truth easily, St. Augustine's prayer is appropriate as we examine some more objections: "I beg you, my God, to show me myself, so that I may confess the fault that is in me to my brethren who will pray for me."[1]

Argument 1:
I still do not see myself as a participant in murder simply because I vote for a pro-choice candidate.

It is difficult to accept such a severe accusation. We think of ourselves as good people and can't visualize ourselves as partners in that kind of murder. After all, we'd never kill another human intentionally.

Dale Carnegie has written that even the most notorious criminals in the worst prisons rationalize their behavior.

Most of them attempt by a form of reasoning, fallacious or logical, to justify their antisocial acts even to themselves, consequently stoutly maintaining that they should have never been imprisoned at all. If Al Capone, Two Gun Crowley, Dutch Schultz, and the other desperate men and women behind prison walls don't blame themselves for anything—what about the people with whom you and I come in contact?[2]

Although most Christians aren't in a class with Al Capone, we have become adept at denial and rationalization. Let's stroll down another path for a few moments—one that doesn't race to the emotional defenses for self-protection and override the reasoning mind. The Texas Penal Code states:

A person commits an offense if he intentionally, knowingly, recklessly, or with criminal negligence, by act or by omission, engages in conduct that places a child younger than fifteen years in imminent danger of death, bodily injury, or physical or mental impairment.[3]

If the defendant had custody of the child, the crime is a second-degree felony and punishable by up to twenty years in prison. If the defendant was not responsible for the child, it is a state jail felony. "An individual adjudged guilty of a state jail felony shall be punished by confinement in a state jail for any term of not more than two years or less than 180 days."[4]

People who vote pro-choice knowingly place 1.3 million children in imminent danger of death. These voters *know* this. Every one of those children will be killed by their mothers and physicians. That means certain death. So people voting pro-choice are guilty of child abuse—a felony offense requiring jail time. Christians must stop the rationalization.

Argument 2:
Ultimately, the women who choose to have an abortion are responsible for the murder, not me.

It's true that the women requesting the abortions bear a *greater* responsibility for murder before God. But isn't the sin of the physician who physically murders the child for pay even greater?

The abortion industry has been immensely successful in their propaganda message that only "tissue" is being aborted. That assuages women's consciences because they're taught that the child inside them isn't a living human person. When women are given the truth with intrauterine photographs showing that the 8-week-old fetus is recognizably human, many change their minds. The physician abortionist, however, *knows* it is a human being.

Prior to 1970, abortions were numbered in the thousands per year. Today, 1.3 million abortions are performed annually. By legalizing the murder of babies, women were *desensitized* to the act of murder that was being performed.

The fact that abortion is now legal is a strong justification for many women. After all, few people would *intentionally* allow the killing of an innocent human being. Many women who do know the truth are desperate and confused about their options when they ask for an abortion. A teenager I know wanted an abortion so that she could complete high school. When she was told that it was possible *not* to kill her baby and still graduate from high school a few months later, she decided to keep her child.

Voting for the pro-choice candidate who champions the choice for abortion murder is like voting for a known terrorist. Imagine that one terrorist promised to give one nuclear bomb every year to a fellow terrorist. The second person would exercise his right to choose to mass murder 1.3 million human beings every year with that bomb. In many confused minds, only the final terrorist is to blame.

Is the political partner of the terrorist who provided the bomb, knowing that millions would die, without blame because his murdering partner had a choice? American law doesn't view it that way and neither does God's Word. Authorizing an act with the known risk of murder is still murder.

According to some U.S. intelligence sources, President Milosovic of Yugoslavia had a legitimate need to remove the Kosovo Liberation Army that was supported by drug smuggling. There is no proof that President Milosovic personally authorized the murder of Albanian civilians and the rape of women: yet, NATO condemned him as a war criminal for his indirect and possibly unintentional crimes. He knew what was occurring through other people by *his* choice. He decided that his priorities and agenda were more important than saving Albanian lives. Is a Christian's decision to vote for a pro-choice candidate any different?

Argument 3:
God knows my heart when I vote—
that is what really matters.

God knows our hearts better than we know them ourselves. But, is He more concerned with our hearts, or our behavior? Can a good heart erase the consequences of sin? Will God exempt us from temporal judgment (here on earth) because our hearts were good?

A person who obeys God's laws, but who doesn't do so from the heart, does not please God. The first commandment is to love the Lord thy God with all of our heart, and soul, and mind, and strength. God looks at our hearts, and if they aren't right, we sin. However, the *heart is not the only area of God's inspection.*[5]

Obedience to God ranks as the highest priority alongside a good heart. *God punishes people for disobedience even if their hearts are good.*

The story of Uzzah in 2 Samuel 6 is a sobering reminder of God's insistence upon obedience. The Philistines had captured the ark of God in battle. King David was bringing it back to Jerusalem on a cart drawn by oxen. The cart was shaken so severely that the ark was in danger of falling off and being damaged. Uzzah, trying to protect the holy ark, reached out with his hand to steady it and prevent it from being damaged.

"And God killed him there for his error, and there he died by the ark of God" (2 Sam. 6:7). King David was angry at God for this act. However, in the Law, God had told the Israelites that the ark was only to be transported by the Levites, who would carry it on long poles. Any person who touched the ark would die. Two men with good hearts did not obey God—one of them died for that sin.

King David was "a man after God's own heart" (Acts 13:22; 1 Sam. 13:14). But when good-hearted King David sinned with Bathsheba and Uriah, God pronounced judgment.

"Thus saith the Lord, Behold I will raise up evil against you out of your own house" (2 Sam. 12:11-12). David's child by Bathsheba died as an infant. Another son committed incest and was killed by a brother. That brother, Absalom, left the country and was estranged from King David, his father, for years. This broke David's heart.

When Absalom finally returned, he revolted against his father and took over the kingdom from David, who was forced to wander the countryside. When Absalom was killed in battle against his father's army, he became the third son to die as a direct result of David's sin.

There are other examples of people in the Bible who are punished even though they were trying to do good. God will punish good-hearted people if they disobey. God expects us to *know* His commandments which He has clearly spoken.

Argument 4:
I can do as much good by voting for other social issues that help people as I can by voting to stop abortion.

The medical principle of triage exposes the fallacy in this argument.

Triage has been depicted in televisions shows such as *M*A*S*H** and *ER*. Medical personnel do a quick survey of the most critically wounded and dying. Those who can last a few hours longer without immediate medical intervention are passed by for those who are near death. The ones closest to death receive our attention first.

Good *can* be done by voting for other issues. It is important to supply hungry children with food and clothing. God *has* commanded it. Welfare *does* help people and may indeed prevent the deaths of some children.[6]

Let's suppose that welfare was completely abolished instantly and 1.3 million children were at risk for dying. We know that these children would live several days, since children survive for months and even years on very little food in third-world countries.

Contrast that with the fact that right now, as you read this book, over four thousand human beings are being killed because abortion murder is legal. The priority belongs to these who are dying immediately. The other children may have other people offer to help when the need gets more desperate.

The care of needy children *is* the Church's responsibility, not the government's job! God has given us, the Church, a direct command to help such children in need. Paying taxes does *not* relieve us of this obligation. How much better it would be if they could receive spiritual food along with the physical food and the loving touch of a human in the name of Jesus who loves them.

Christians are already providing this higher quality welfare in other countries through organizations like Catholic Charities, Compassion International and World Vision. These relief organizations provide food, clothing, and education for hundreds of thousands of children in third-world countries. Isn't it reasonable to think that Christians would take the lead in providing for our *own* children here in America?

There are other important social issues such as education, the environment, taxes, minority rights, women's rights, the economy, etc. However, these are not immediate needs–their absence doesn't threaten imminent death. All of these good causes combined cannot surpass the value of four thousand human beings who are murdered every day here in America to help another "good" cause. We still have time to make *God's* priority *our* priority.

Argument 5:
I have prayed about this and I do not believe that voting pro-choice (to kill babies and harm women) is a sin.

Praying is one of several components to determine God's will. It does work, provided that the foundation of the Scriptures has been laid in the heart.

Many sincere Christians have prayed for God's direction in their lives, but then blatantly disobeyed His commands in the Scriptures. God has given us His principles in writing because the heart is deceitfully wicked (Jer. 17:9-10).

I have been unable to find anyplace in the Bible that encourages us to pray in order to distinguish what is sin. All that we need to know about sin has been written in the principles of the Scriptures. We only need to pray for God to expose it in our lives.

According to 2 Timothy 3:16, "All Scripture is given by inspiration of God and is profitable for doctrine, for reproof, for correction, for instruction in righteousness, so that the man of God may be proficient for every good work." In 2 Timothy 2:15, believers are advised to "Study to show yourself approved unto God, a workman that does not need to be ashamed, rightly dividing the Word of truth."

As R.C. Sproul has said, "To be conformed to Jesus, we must first begin to think as Jesus did. . . . That cannot happen without a mastery of His Word."[7]

Using prayer to determine sin has been *disastrous* in God's Church. I know a woman in my local church who prayed about divorcing her husband. She proudly announced one winter that God had told her she could divorce him as His Christmas present to her. It did not matter that Malachi 2:16 clearly states that God hates divorce. It did not matter that Jesus clearly said that divorce was not permitted except for adultery (Matt. 5:32). This woman concluded that God had made a special exception for her, because she had prayed about it. There was no adultery on his part—no abuse. She had *no* biblical reason for the divorce. She was deceiving herself.

God gave us His Holy Scriptures so that we can have every principle we need to live in a way that pleases Him. Do you want to know about sin? Read the Book.

Fetal Fortune

Prayer can even reap profits off of the harvesting of fetal parts. Brenda Bardsley, President of AGF, sees nothing wrong with providing fetal parts to researchers. She attends a conservative church in Georgia and even homeschools her three children. "I've been painted as this monster, but here I am trying to give my kids a Christian education," she said. "Mrs. Bardsley says she has prayed over whether her business is acceptable in God's sight, and had 'got the feeling' that it is."[8]

She even teaches her children that abortion is wrong. Yet, she can bring in revenues of millions of dollars a year harvesting fetal parts. What is the old saying about children doing what we *do*, and not what we *say*? Yes, those children *are* receiving an education—but it is certainly *not* Christian!

The Biblical Conscience

Prayer has become an easy way for us to convince ourselves that God agrees with our plans. This type of prayer to discover sin merely exposes our inept consciences. Conscience is no longer a reliable guide to right and wrong. Chuck Colson wrote a *Breakpoint* article on 16 November 1999, entitled "Counterfeit Conscience."

> This is what people have in mind when they say, for example, "My conscience does not tell me that abortion is wrong, therefore abortion is not wrong for me." What they mean is, "I don't feel bad about it, so it's not wrong."[9]

Philosopher Russell Hittinger analyzes this "neo-conscience" as a reduction to "the writer of permission slips" for immoral behavior.

Chuck Colson accurately explains the result:

> In other words, in the absence of moral leadership and example, people lose a sense of duty, and abandon themselves to their own autonomous choices. But the good news is that, by the same token, leadership can help restore a proper definition of duty and conscience. Not a king as in Old Testament times, but the leadership of godly men and women in the church.[10]

I know Christians who love God but commit serious sins due to their lack of knowledge of God's Word. We can also believe a lie because it better fits what we want to do. When God's truth is demonstrated from the Scriptures, we can conveniently relegate it to personal opinion. Post-modernism is alive and well in the Church in America.

We must seek God's clear principles of sin in His written Word. When we try to identify sin by prayer, we are acting as dangerously as a pilot who flies the plane through a thick fog—by relying on his feelings about the right direction.

A pilot must forget feelings of the direction and rely solely on the instruments.

God's Word is our navigational instrument when it comes to sin.

Conclusions

An honest answer to the four key questions reveals whether or not we have strongholds—areas protected from God that block us from seeing His truth. Even "good" Christians can rationalize selfish behavior. Furthermore, we often do not see what we do not *want* to see. Much may be at stake personally.

God does know our hearts better than we do. But He judges our obedience as well as our hearts. We should not attempt to place the blame for the millions of murders on someone else because they are *more* responsible. We, too, must accept responsibility.

Other social issues are important. None, however, can compare with the forty-six million murders of innocent unborn humans worldwide each year. The devaluing of human life heralds a frightening culture of death that will only increase.

We should not pray to determine if something is a sin. Today's average American Christian conscience is inadequate; but God's Word is sufficient to lead us into all truth. The principles are all there. If we study His Book, God's Spirit will show us the answer.

Notes

1. St. Augustine of Hippo, *The Confessions of St. Augustine* (New York: New American Library, 1963), 251.

2. Carnegie, D., *How to Win Friends and Influence People* (Simon & Schuster, 1981), 33.

3. Texas Penal Code, Title 5, Offenses Against the Person, Section §22.04.1. Abandoning or endangering a child; accessed 27 February 2000; available from www.cowtown.net/Cop_Shop/chapter_22.html.

4. Ibid., Title 3, Punishments, Section §12.35. State jail felony punishments.

5. This verse in 1 Samuel 16 is often misunderstood: "For man looks on the outward appearance but God looks on the heart." The first part of the verse provides the context and meaning. "Do not look on his outward beauty or how tall he is, because I have rejected

him." The context is a man whom Samuel thought would make a good king because he was handsome and tall. God stated that the heart was more important than the physical looks. This passage cannot be used to say that the motives of the heart are more important than actions. God does *not* say that the heart is more important than actions—only physical looks.

6. Our present governmental welfare of the past forty years has been inept at truly helping the poor despite billions of dollars spent. The Personal Responsibility and Work Opportunity Reconciliation Act of 1996 was a good step toward correcting the problem. Why? Because it is patterned after *biblical* welfare. People who could work were required to work in order to receive food. It was not brought to their doorstep. See Leviticus 19:9. Also, Deanna Carlson, of The Family Research Council in Washington, D.C., has written a book entitled, *The Welfare of My Neighbor: Living Out Christ's Love for the Poor.*

7. Sproul, R.C., *The Holiness of God,* 164.

8. Vincent, L., "The Harvest of Abortion," *World* (23 October 1999): 16-19.

9. Colson, C., "Counterfeit Conscience," *Breakpoint* (15 November 1999).

10. Ibid.

18.

Words Win the Debate

At an Oregon Medical Association meeting that I attended, the physicians were voting on a resolution to change just one word. The insurance companies' contracts had replaced the word "physician" with the word "provider." A physician rose to speak, and pointed out that even a criminal drug dealer could be called a "provider"—we were medical doctors.

Why did he make a big fuss over one word? Because terms mean everything. Physicians are supposed to develop relationships of trust and compassion with their patients, not be vendors of medical supplies and equipment. Whoever controls the terms wins the debate.

At that same meeting, a heated debate began when one county medical society wanted to provide all sexually active women with a "morning after pill" directly from pharmacies. One of their reasons was to bypass the heated debate over abortions. By making this pill available, abortions could be minimized.

There was only one problem. Several of us delegates took to the microphone reminding these doctors that we would *still* be advocating abortion. Even though it was not a surgical abortion, it was still an abortion by the use of a drug. Intelligent doctors suddenly realized their mistake.

Words Are Critical

Perhaps in reading this book you have been annoyed at my constant insertion of clarifying words after the term "pro-choice" (to kill humans and harm women.) This is by design: words are critical. Word games like *useless eaters*, *hereditary worth*, and the *final solution* were popularized in Germany to hide the millions dying in the Holocaust.

Abortion has been redefined as the termination of pregnancy. In the popular fiction series by Tim LaHaye and Jerry Jenkins, this problem is addressed in *The Rise of Antichrist— NICOLAE*. Rayford points this out to Hattie:

> "And of course, I can terminate the pregnancy."
>
> "What does that mean exactly?"
>
> "What do you mean 'what does that mean?' " Hattie had said. "Terminate the pregnancy means terminate the pregnancy."
>
> "You mean have an abortion?"
>
> Hattie had stared at him like he was an imbecile.
>
> "Yes! What did you think I meant?"
>
> "Well, it just seems you're using language that makes it sound like the easiest option."
>
> . . . "Hattie, just humor me for a moment and assume that the pregnancy, that 'it' you're carrying, is already a child."[1]

People are not moved to compassion by terminating a pregnancy. Isn't that like terminating a contract or a deal? When you hear this phrase, politely interject, "You mean kill the baby?"

That Media Thing You Do

The media has been particularly deceptive in their controlling use of sanctity of life terms. They know that whoever controls the terms wins the debate.

So you won't think I'm a paranoid radical, let me quote two respected Christians who feel this way. The first is Pope John Paul II:

> Nor can it be denied that the mass media are often implicated in this conspiracy, by lending credit to this culture which presents recourse to contraception, sterilization, abortion, and even euthanasia as a mark of progress and a victory of freedom, while depicting as enemies of freedom and progress those positions which are unreservedly pro-life.[2]

The second statement is by Billy Graham: "Almost without exception, the media have staunchly defended a woman's right to abortion. One of the few meaningful expressions of disapproval I have found in any newspaper is . . . An editorial in the Orlando, Florida, *Sentinel.*"[3]

Two separate opinion polls revealed that the average journalist opposes God's priorities. Ninety percent supported a woman's right to kill her child by abortion, and 86 percent seldom or never attend church or synagogue—only 20 percent are Protestant, 14 percent practicing Jews, and 13 percent Catholic.[4] Only 2 percent identify themselves as conservative.[5]

With the media controlling the terms, it is more difficult to educate the public and teach the truth. The media will not be won until public opinion is won. Remember what Abraham Lincoln said, "Public sentiment is everything."[6]

Therefore, it is up to Christians to speak the truth in love. We should not attack them with accusations—they are deceived. I like my Christian brother's explanation about his calm response when homosexuals were disrupting his church services.

A reporter asked Ron Greer, "How can you be so controlled—you're not angry?"

Ron replied, "I could no more be angry at them than a blind man who stepped on my foot."[7]

One way we can demonstrate God's love is to befriend local journalists. We can educate and implore them to look closely at this holocaust. As relationships become trusted, we can tell those outside of Christ's Church about God's holiness, our sin, and His forgiveness in Jesus Christ. If we profess to follow Jesus Christ in loving our neighbor, we cannot do otherwise.

Abortion Redefined

Have you ever noticed how the pregnant mother who *wants* the child calls it a "baby" from the very start? Yet, the mother who does not want it will refer to a *fetus* or *it* or *the pregnancy.* It's amazing how an arbitrary word change can spell life or death to the same baby.

I believe that the neutral term "abortion" should not be used. This act is murder from God's point of view. *What* are we aborting? The launch of the space shuttle? The computer program?

We're talking about aborting a human life—killing a human person. So, instead of *abortion*, the term should be "abortion killing." *Abortion killing* correctly emphasizes who is being terminated—a living human being. *Abortion killing* forces the listener back to reality.

I have chosen the word "killing" for a good reason. Our society isn't ready to hear that abortion is murder. We have much educating to do. But when we're speaking to Christians, I believe we should use the term "abortion murder." God's biblical truth helps explain this term. That will go a long way in helping us Christians recapture the horror of abortion murder.

Let's not use this term to condemn people. Remember that it is a Christian woman who requests one out of every six abortions. But, the use of *abortion killing* will help us grasp this suppressed truth that we as the Church have ignored.

Anti-Abortion

A newspaper in Los Angeles, California won't allow journalists to use the word "pro-life" in their articles.[8] It's always changed to "anti-abortion." As you know, it is unpopular to be anti-*anything* these days.

When you read or hear the term "anti-abortion," try responding this way: "I'm not anti-abortion, I'm anti-killing. You can abort as many computer programs as you desire. I'm opposed to killing humans."

Anti-killing brings the result of the abortion murder back to the table for discussion: humans are being killed.

Pro-Choice to Kill

The term "pro-choice" has also contributed to the 38 million murders. When we use this term, we're not referring to which dress to wear or which sport event to attend. We mean the choice—the mother's "right"—to kill the baby inside of her. The phrase should be, "pro-choice to kill humans." This correctly places the emphasis on the absurdity that we should have the choice to kill another person. This phrase forces the listener to consider that her choice kills a person. A child *will die* as a result of her choice.

The damage to women resulting from abortion murder—both physically (sometimes including death) and psychologically—has been extensively documented. Therefore, the term *pro-choice* should be used only with the additional clarifying words "pro-choice to kill humans and harm women." If these clarifying terms are unpleasant to us as Christians, it means we've been brainwashed.

Some people will want to change the phrase to "pro-choice to *allow* killing humans" or "pro-choice to *authorize* killing humans." These statements are both true. However, I prefer the simpler statement: "pro-choice to kill humans." This will help to remind us that God's view of participation in murder demands a higher standard than we have in America today. We are choosing to participate in murder when we vote for a pro-choice over a pro-life candidate.

"Freedom of choice" should be handled in the same way: "Freedom to choose to kill another person."

Health of the Mother

We learned in a previous chapter about the origin of this deceptive phrase. Who can argue with protecting the "health of the mother"?

Our position is that we should protect the life of the mother, just as we protect the life of the other human whom she carries inside her. We must press this point to those who argue for the "health" exception. If they're in doubt, we can ask: "Would you be willing to let me kill you for the sake of my health?"

While we're discussing health, don't be fooled by the claim that "back-alley coat-hanger abortions" were killing thousands of women a year prior to the legalization of abortion. After the introduction of penicillin, maternal deaths dropped from 1,679 in 1940 to 316 deaths in 1950.[9] The U.S. Bureau of Vital Statistics report in 1983 proves that this rate remained fairly constant for decades—there were 128 deaths in 1970. Every death is tragic. That is why it is so tragic that no stringent requirements exist for the reporting of deaths from women having abortions today. These deaths can be "hidden" by reporting them under other causes, such as hemorrhage and infection, although they resulted from an abortion.[10]

Pro-choice really does kill humans and harm women.

Every Child a Wanted Child

Let's complete the sentence the way a pro-choice candidate or voter would end it.

"Every child a wanted child; and if not wanted, then killed."

Millions of childless couples long to adopt children; therefore, every child is wanted by *someone*. In addition, contrary to current propaganda, abortion does not prevent child abuse. Over 90 percent of abuse is committed by parents who wanted their children—they were planned pregnancies.[11] Child abuse has skyrocketed 600 percent since abortion on demand was legalized in 1973; and, the experts admit that increased reporting cannot explain this tragedy. [12, 13] Abortion is the ultimate form of child abuse.

Neither is abortion the answer to overpopulation. Killing off the "extras" is terrifying. Billy Graham makes this clear:

> I have heard some people say, "Well, I'm against abortion, but with the population crisis and all the unwanted child-birth in the world, especially among the poor, abortion is probably for the best." Let me be quick to say that this kind of reasoning is false and dangerous. . . . We can demonstrate God's love, but we must never think that we can solve one moral crisis by condoning another, especially the crime of murder, for unrestrained abortion is nothing less that that.[14]

Personally Opposed to Abortion

To say one is personally opposed to abortion is illogical and unsupportable. It undermines the foundation of natural law and order in society. You will hear many people echo the favorite political phrase, "I'm personally opposed to abortion." Ask them if they support your desire to kill another human being.

Keep in mind what Abraham Lincoln, who had a way of pushing through the smokescreen of words, said about such "personally opposed" arguments: "Whenever I hear anyone arguing for slavery, I feel a strong impulse to see it tried on him personally."[15]

Some people will try to make the argument that if pro-life advocates had their way, women would be jailed for paying for an abortion. This is another smokescreen. Not a single woman was ever convicted and jailed in America for having an abortion when it was illegal. Doctors were convicted and jailed.[16] As Susan B. Anthony stated, "We want prevention, not prosecution."[17]

The Pill

The medical doctors, at the state meeting mentioned earlier, erred in their understanding of what constitutes an abortion. Unless we educate ourselves, so will we.

The Oregonian newspaper, speaking of RU-486, subtly influences us this way:

> The abortion drug, available in Europe for more than 11 years, could soon be available to American women wanting to end their pregnancies.[18]

> The drug, also known as mifepristone, works by blocking the effects of progesterone, a hormone necessary to maintain pregnancy. Two days after taking the pill, the woman must return to her doctor's office to take a hormone called misoprostol, which causes uterine contractions to expel the fetus. (Ibid.)

> For antiabortion activists, the bottom line is clear: Medical abortion, induced by a drug, is still abortion. (Ibid.)

Did you notice the terms: "end their pregnancies," "expel the fetus," and "antiabortion activists?"

The same paper displays a photograph from January 1998 outside the U.S. Supreme Court Building. Demonstrators are marching with the National Abortion Rights Action League (NARAL) with placards declaring "I'm pro-choice and I pray" (Ibid.). It's a sad commentary on media brainwashing and biblical illiteracy. Individuals who are pro-choice had better pray—pray in repentance, asking God for forgiveness.

The abortion pill has the same effect as the operation: It

kills. The "morning after pill" sounds like a remedy for a hangover. But it kills a human, so we should call it "the killer pill." Although rare, this *killer pill* could also result in the death of the mother from bleeding. In a controlled study published in the *New England Journal of Medicine*, one out of a hundred women required blood transfusions or an operation.[19]

The Pill Kills Embryos

These pills only reliably kill humans in the late embryo and early fetal stage. "Embryo" is a term that will become more common as more medical abortions using medications are provided. This refers to a human up to the eighth or ninth week in development. The fingers and the hands have already formed and the embryo looks human.

Embryo and *fetus* are merely different ways to describe a human person. It would be like saying *newborn, infant, teenager,* or *senior citizen.* The embryo is a person. This can be demonstrated by the legal adoption of frozen embryos. These embryos are then implanted in the mother's womb by *in vitro* fertilization and she carries the child to term. Christian Adoption and Family Services has developed a Snowflakes Embryo Adoption Program for legally adopting frozen children like these.[20] They should not be discarded.

Conclusions

Do not be brainwashed by the media. They are willing accomplices in perpetuating the deaths of millions. Words win the debate. We must challenge the terms in order to clarify them:

- Abortion killing
- Pro-choice to kill humans and harm women
- Freedom to choose to kill
- Personally opposed to killing
- Anti-killing
- The killer pill

Speak the truth in love to those outside of the Church. Challenge the abuse of terms that hides this present holocaust. The responsibility rests upon us who follow Jesus Christ.

Notes

1. LaHaye, T., and Jerry B. Jenkins, *The Rise of the Antichrist NICOLAE* (Wheaton, IL: Tyndale House Publishers, 1997), 294-296.

2. Pope John Paul II, *Evangelium Vitae* 1995, 696.

3. Graham, B., *Storm Warning*, 235.

4. Lichter, S., and Rothman, S., "The Media Elite: White, Male, Secular, and Liberal," *Public Opinion*, 1981.

5. Lenoski, E., Heartbeat, vol. 3, no. 4 (December 1980), quoted by Dr. and Mrs. J.C. Wilke in *Why Can't We Love Them Both?* (Cincinnati, OH: Hayes Publishing company, 1997), 258.

6. McKenna, G., "On Abortion," *Atlantic Monthly*, 61.

7. Personal communication with author, 17 October 1999.

8. The *Los Angeles Times* and other newspapers have this policy, even if "unofficial."

9. U.S. Bureau of Vital Statistics, Center for Disease Control, from the U.S. Senate debate on the Hatch-Eagleton Pro-life Amendment in 1983 as quoted by John C. Wilke, M.D., *Why Can't We Love Them Both?* (Cincinnati, OH: Hayes Publishing Company, 1997), 156.

10. Ibid., 148-149.

11. Lenoski, E., Heartbeat, vol. 3, no. 4 (December 1980), as cited by Dr. and Mrs. J.C. Wilke, M.D., *Why Can't We Love Them Both?* (Cincinnati, OH: Hayes Publishing Company, 1997), 258.

12. U.S. Department of Health and Human Services, National Center of Child Abuse, Child Maltreatment, 1997. The rate was 167,000 in 1973 when abortion was legalized, then jumped to 711,142 within six years—a 430 percent increase. The past twenty years has seen a 200 percent increase. A similar increase in abuse occurred in Canada with abortion between 1971 and 1994, according to the Child Welfare Branch, Ministry of Human Resources, Ontario, Canada.

13. Ney, P., "Relationship Between Abortion and Child Abuse," Canadian Journal of Psychiatry, vol. 24 (1979): 610-620. This ar-

ticle was published from the University of British Columbia. It explains that abortion lowers a parent's resistance to violence and abuse of their children who are born.

14. Graham, B., *Storm Warning,* 236. His subheading is entitled, "The Abortion Holocaust."

15. Lincoln, A., 17 March 1865 as quoted in *Bartlett's Familiar Quotations* (Boston: Little, Brown, and Company, 1863, 1980), 524.

16. Olasky, M., *Abortion Rites: A Social History of Abortion in America* (Wheaton, IL: Crossway Books, 1992), 157, 228-229, 234.

17. Anthony, S.B., as quoted by the Susan B. Anthony Foundation radio advertisement, 18 February 2000 on KBVM, Portland, Oregon.

18. Palmer, L., "RU-486: Changing the debate," *The Oregonian* (7 January 2000): A16.

19. Silvester, et. al., "Interruption of Pregnancy with Mifepristone (RU-486) and a Prostaglandin Analogue," *New England Journal of Medicine,* vol. 322, no. 10 (8 March 1990): 645-648.

20. Neven, T., *Focus on the Family Physician* (Colorado Springs, CO: Physicians Resource Council—*Focus on the Family,* January 2000): 11-12.

The Clock Is Ticking for America

Values in American culture have shifted. Older tradition-alists and modernists are dying. Younger "Cultural Creatives" reject absolute values. Quoting from an article in *American Demographics* magazine, Chuck Colson and Nancy Pearcey explain further:

> Individuals in the fast-growing Cultural Creatives group tend to be young, well-educated, affluent, and assertive. Interestingly, six out of ten are women. They are on the cutting edge of social change, and if they are not already the dominant influence, they soon will be.[1]

Without moral absolutes, the postmodern, autonomous individualist is drawn to hedonism like a fish on a line. Whether or not they accept Christ or Christianity, they must be taught that God, who is personal and has expectations of us, is our Creator. Without *this* absolute as the starting point, all other philosophies will lead to a violent disrespect for human life.

God often allows rebellious people and nations to self-destruct. Billy Graham warns of this inevitable judgment upon our own nation unless we repent.

"Even history declares the tragic legacy of promiscuous societies from Carthage and Rome to Renaissance France. And the Bible declares repeatedly the wrath of God on those who persist in such sin."[2]

Francis Schaeffer warned that America was racing to a self-destruction predicted over two hundred years ago:

> Edward Gibbon (1737-1794) in his *Decline and Fall of the Roman Empire* (1776-1788) said that the following five attributes marked Rome at its end: first, a mounting love

of show and luxury (that is, affluence); second, a widening gap between the very rich and the very poor (this could be among countries in the families of nations as well as in a single nation); third, an obsession with sex; fourth, freakishness in the arts, masquerading as originality, and enthusiasms pretending to be creativity; fifth, an increased desire to live off the state. It all sounds so familiar.[3]

God's Wrath on Men

Tolerance has become the highest virtue in the cultural elite of America. It has also affected Christians. But God hasn't switched His view because society has changed.

This Holy God pronounced judgment upon sin and destroyed nations. Jesus called people "beautiful caskets full of bones from decaying corpses" (Matt. 23:27). He also pronounced the judgment of mass death upon sinners, and predicted the destruction of Israel's temple *because* of their sin. Today, Jesus would probably be sent for "sensitivity training."

Two millennia ago, a religious community voted to kill an innocent person for the "good" of the nation. Before his death, Jesus Christ prophesied that the nation of Israel would be destroyed within *one* generation (forty years is a biblical generation) for the killing of innocent prophets as well as Himself. His prophecy was fulfilled in 70 A.D., when one million Jews were killed by Titus' Roman army (Luke 13:1-5); and not one stone of the temple was left standing (Matt. 23:35-24:2).[4]

God physically punishes individuals and sinning nations— even if it is God's *own* people who fail to confess their sin and return to Him. Christians must turn back to God and stop the killing of innocent humans before God punishes us with calamity. When pouring out His wrath upon nations, forty years has been a popular time period. If He follows this pattern, we don't have much time remaining to stop the legalized mass murder of the unborn.

The Idol of Choice

One of the major accusations of God against Israel was the sacrifice of their newborn babies to the heathen god, Molech. The babies were placed live into the intense fire of Molech's burning hands by the parents who were not allowed to show emotion. This is a close parallel to the thousands of partial birth abortions being committed in America. Ezekiel 23:39 seems to fit: "For when they had slain their children to their idols, then they came the same day into my sanctuary to profane it."

Today, we worship a new idol: women sacrifice their babies in order to *re*gain control of their bodies. Maybe we haven't progressed very far in twenty-five hundred years. We are the generation that has sacrificed millions of our unborn babies to our idols of personal comfort, affluence, and choice.

Unless the leadership of the Church accepts its responsibility to teach and confront sin among us, we will never be the Church that God calls us to be. I agree with Cardinal O'Connor who believes that the Church holds the key to stopping abortion on demand in America. It's time that we took a stand—isn't it?

How Long Can We Wait?

A local church in Portland, Oregon had been supportive of Advocates for Life as they peaceably demonstrated outside an abortion clinic. Pro-choice activists retaliated by running up the church aisles and throwing condoms to disrupt the service. The ACLU helped sue and won a multimillion dollar settlement against a key member. Many members left as a result of the weekly demonstrations.[5]

Is this a warning to churches that become involved in the moral issue of abortion? Yes. It is a sobering consideration because it deters our ability to preach the gospel. This warning should be heeded.

So, if leaders teach that a vote for a pro-choice candidate is a sin, does it place that church at the same risk? I do not believe that it does. This disaster and similar incidents are not analogous to the present considerations.

Why? This local church supported Advocates for Life—this was *not* a religious organization. AFL was a moral activist group that peaceably demonstrated at abortion clinics. The church was hit and a member sued over a moral issue that was nonreligious in the mind of the ACLU.

Many churches openly support Crisis Pregnancy Centers. These nonreligious organizations take a moral stand on a political issue, as did Advocates for Life. Such churches face the same risk with this position. The ACLU could possibly sue the local church for using funds for nonreligious, political purposes.

Unfortunately, the pagan world can make claims to moral issues just as easily as the Church can claim moral grounds. Political interests could easily be confused with such activism and vague moral issues.

But the question we face is not merely a moral issue–it is a sin issue. Does a vote for a supporter of mass murder of babies constitute a sin? Yes, we have shown that biblical principles clearly make this case.

Sin remains the sole domain of God's Church. The ACLU or the media would have a more difficult task covering sin as being political.[6] We can be sure, however, they will continue to push all sin issues as political. Why should Satan's forces stop a winning strategy?

We cannot continue to ignore our responsibility as Christ's Church. We must teach all nations to obey all things that He has commanded. If we don't, the way Christians are increasingly being pushed down legally, we'll eventually be forbidden by law to preach all things that Christ has commanded.

The recent ruling in December 1999, by the Federal Communications Commission against a Christian television station, has been further proof. These elitists have declared that "worship services do not contribute to the educational and cultural needs of the public."[7] This broadcaster's license and hundreds of others given to smaller television broadcasters were suspended. How far do we let it go before it is no longer "political?" How long can we wait?

Another Storm Warning

In 1999, Gloria Feldt, President of Planned Parenthood, mailed out letters that accused Christian organizations of murder and violence. Her letter asserted:

> Considering that many current members of Congress feel their political base is represented by religious political extremist groups like Pat Robertson's Christian Coalition,

and lesser-known organizations like Gary Bauer's Family Research Council and James Dobson's Focus on the Family. . . . All of these groups are politically astute, extremely well funded, and have a fanatical—often militant— approach to achieving their goals. . . . To some of these groups, this might mean bombing a clinic . . . blockading a door . . . harassing a patient . . . Stalking a doctor.[8]

The progressive pattern of persecution that history has followed can be seen right here in America. It begins with public ridicule—portraying ministers and priests as dishonest, ignorant hypocrites on television series and in films. The next step is to marginalize the group, especially politically. They are removed from political office because "they do not belong there." It should come as no surprise that the Church has been labeled as "extremists" or the "radical right" or "religious zealots," and instructed to stay out of politics.

Victimization follows so that this group is not protected equally by law. A homosexual man was tragically killed in Montana and the hate crime received widespread attention across America. But when a dozen Christians were shot while worshipping at Wedgewood Baptist Church in Texas (September 1999), no hate crime could be found among the many dead bodies. The law applies differently to different people. Are Christians being marched toward the final stage?

In the final stage, open persecution stomps down every semblance of true Christian teaching, leaving only the two covers of an empty Bible for people to worship. Some may label this sensationalism, but the signs are progressive and consistent. As George Barna tells us, "Without a visible witness to the contrary, the mass media will continue to portray churches and Christianity negatively, while giving positive affirmation to the new strains of religions and religious leaders competing for America's souls."[9]

Compromising Leaves Us Compromised

In Canada, where Christians stayed out of politics, Romans 1:18-32 can no longer be taught or preached on the radio. That's the passage where God plainly declares the sexual practice of homosexuality to be a sin. Christians can no longer teach the whole Gospel. It is against the law to call homosexuality a sin.[10]

This has also occurred in Britain where religious programs are now prohibited from obtaining a radio license. The *Christian Daily News* quoted Edward Leigh of the British Parliament in 1999 as saying, "One can get a national radio license to promote atheism, but one is prevented by law from promoting Christianity."[11]

Why are these things happening? Because Christians abandoned their obligation to teach all that Christ commanded. This compromise to refrain from teaching *all* nations to obey *all* things has been accepted. The teaching of salvation in Christ is seen to be more important than teaching that the sexual practice of homosexuality is a sin. At first glance, that may appear to be true.

But where does this precarious compromise end? Mankind must know that they are sinners in the eyes of God before they can realize their *need for the Savior.* God *does* love homosexuals, but they are at risk both now and eternally. If we cannot tell them they are sinners, they will not know their need for the Savior! Where does the gospel end and the political begin?

Compromising essential issues places us in a compromised position more than just politically.

The Compromised Church

A church leader told me that knowingly voting for an immoral man was a sin. However, he does not see voting for a pro-choice candidate as sin. How can this be? The answer is: "It's politics."

Candidates can pick and choose their unique positions on multiple issues. What if a candidate was faithful to his wife, did not take bribes, told the truth, and was honest in his dealings, but *voluntarily* voted to allow the mass murder of 1.3 million humans every year? Would he or she be a moral or an immoral person?

Isn't mass murder the epitome of violence and sin? We need to rethink our arbitrary line that we have drawn to separate the Church and politics. Christian compromise is leading us down the dangerous street of retribution from both God and man.

Theodore Roosevelt is known more as a great President than a prophet. Yet, the following quote establishes some credibility for the latter:

> Progress has brought us both unbounded opportunities and unbridled difficulties. Thus, the measure of our civilization will not be that we have done much, but what we have done with that much. I believe that the next half century will advance the cause of Christian civilization or revert to the horrors of brutal paganism. . . . The choice between the two is upon us.[12]

Aleksander Solzhenitsyn, who knew about persecution, was critical of our Western culture. In a foreword to Solzhenitsyn's book, *The Oak and the Calf*, Alonzo L. McDonald wrote:

> He concluded that spiritual life was destroyed in the East by the ruling party and in the West by commercial interests. . . . Naturally, his critics multiplied as his writings threatened all special and powerful interests—including church leaders and pacifists in the West—whom he accused of knowing of nothing in life worth dying for.[13]

Conclusions

Many in the younger generation know only relative values—not absolute morals. They will be in control of America in the not too distant future. Will we take a stand to teach the foundation of God as Creator once again, and to reinstate His Ten Commandments?

How long can we wait before God's judgment falls? Will we suffer the consequences of our own neglect and be rendered unable to teach God's whole gospel like our Canadian neighbors?

The Church in America had better figure out what is "worth dying for." For what are we willing to die? With the rapid progress in the persecution pattern, we may have to answer that question sooner than we think. The clock is ticking for America.

Notes

1. Colson, C., and Nancy Pearcey, *How Now Shall We Live?*, 25-26.

2. Graham, B., *Storm Warning*, 235.

3. Schaeffer, F., *The Complete Works of Francis Schaeffer. A Christian Worldview*, vol. 5, *A Christian View of the West*, 227.

4. Josephus, R., *The War of the Jews* 6.9.1, 6.9.3, translated by Whiston, W., *Josephus: The Complete Works* (Nashville, TN: Thomas Nelson, 1998), 897-898.

5. Personal correspondence with Bob Cryder several times during the fall of 1998. Bob was a former member of the Church for twelve years.

6. The present governmental system and media continue to push homosexuality as a political agenda. This is clearly sin according to Romans 1. We must not allow them to push all of God's commandments out of the realm of the Church, one by one. If we allow them, they will certainly do it, just like the Third Reich pushed the true Church out of German society.

7. Editorial, *The Wall Street Journal* (19 January 2000): A-22. This was a ruling by Chairman William Kennard of the FCC (order #99-393) against Cornerstone—a Christian, noncommercial, educational television group.

8. Feldt, G., Planned Parenthood Federation of America, Inc. Newsletter (December 1999): 1-2.

9. Barna, G., *The Second Coming of the Church*, 208.

10. *Ottawa Citizen* (5 November 1997): 17. Quoted by "Focus on the Family Newsletter," June 1998.

11. Christian News Service, September 1999, quoted by Coral Ridge Ministries Newsletter (October 1999), 7.

12. Roosevelt, T., 1909, as quoted by George Grant, *The Quick and the Dead* (Wheaton, IL: Crossway Books, 1981), 134.

13. Solzhenitsyn, A.L., *The Oak and the Calf* (Burke, VA: The Trinity Forum, 1992), 5.

20.

Putting Faith to Work

Since the clock is ticking, hopefully no Christian will object to us putting our faith to work. But how do we go about it? It reminds me of a quote by Thomas Merton on contemplation:

> One of the worst things about an ill-timed effort to share the knowledge of contemplation with other people is that you assume that everybody else will want to see things from your point of view when, as a matter of fact, they will not. They will raise objections to everything that you say, and you will find yourself in a theological controversy—or worse, a pseudo-scientific one.[1]

The Individual Approach

We are all different in abilities, giftedness, and callings. The Church is supposed to function like a coordinated physical body—each person performing important tasks as we all work together (1 Cor. 12:11-31). Since we are all different, we shouldn't approach others in exactly the same way. We should take our lead from Jesus. He didn't point a finger at the woman at the well, and say accusingly, "You committed adultery with six men." Instead, He talked gently with her while still confronting her sin.[2] Yet, Jesus was critical of the religious leaders. He called them hypocrites and warned of judgment. People in leadership, who should know better, are *more* responsible before God.

Shouting "murderer" to a non-Christian abortionist is unlikely to result in either a spiritual or a moral conversion. Remember, those outside of Christ are blinded. We must educate them with truth as we demonstrate love. They do need to understand their sin, but let's begin with fetology and natural law before we attack them with the sword of God's Holy Scriptures.

On the other hand, Christians need to know that God considers abortion and euthanasia to be murder. Many don't know, so let's teach them from God's Word. Until they see the unborn as our neighbor who is made in God's image, they will not care if millions of the unborn die.

The leaders of the Church must also be educated about the deception of spiritual isolation. God desires us to preach the *whole* gospel—physical care of the needy and rescuing those who are condemned to die. The spiritual spines of leaders must be strengthened like steel to model God's priority of life. We must have the courage to do what is right, even if it costs us.

Many Christian leaders have been afraid to show pictures depicting these unborn neighbors—afraid to "carefront" sin from the pulpits. Women have chosen not to kill their unborn babies in large part because of leaders who have had the courage to speak out, educate, show pictures of our neighbors in the womb, and offer help.

The mass killing of the American unborn will stop by one-to-one communication and education. The individual approach will work.

Education

Educating our youth is critical. This country cannot survive without God's foundation. We are not trying to impose a theocratic Christian government upon America any more than the founding fathers did.[3] However, we must bring God back into the classrooms—just as they did. Our Creator, who endowed us with unalienable rights, deserves some airtime to explain *His* view of life, liberty, and the pursuit of happiness.

Since *Edwards v. Aguillard* in 1987, the teaching of God as Creator has been replaced by naturalistic evolution.[4] Our children have been brainwashed that God did not create anything. Chance plus time equals everything—including our human lives. If that's true, human life is no more valuable than the life of a worm. No wonder we have a problem. Our children are acting on what we have taught them, both in the classroom and in the abortion clinics of America.

"Thou shalt not kill" must be put back on classroom walls. It still stands etched upon our historic buildings, along with the other Ten Commandments. Since God's law was removed in 1980 (*Stone v. Graham*),[5] we have witnessed anarchy. We shouldn't be surprised that Colorado's homeschool rate increased 10 percent the year following the Columbine killings. Even the *Wall Street Journal* portrays homeschooling as a good alternative.[6]

Public educators need to push the administrators for moral absolutes. Parents must demand that God be allowed in the classroom to preserve these moral absolutes. As Francis Schaeffer warned, "If there are no absolutes by which to judge society, then society is absolute."[7] When society is absolute, the arbitrary will of the majority may then kill any minority. When society is absolute, a totalitarian state must eventually rescue the disorder of hedonism. Returning to an education based upon natural law will start us down the path to recovery.

Dr. William Bennett has written about the tremendous success that Christian based education has achieved for America's disadvantaged, the urban poor and non-Catholics, especially non-Catholic black and Hispanic students.

> In New York City, according to *Time* magazine, Catholic schools graduate 99 percent of their students on time, while public schools graduate 38 percent of their students on time. Catholic schools educate at a cost of $1,735 per student, while public schools spend over $7,000 per student. The average public school teacher in New York City makes just under $44,000 per year, while the average Catholic-schoolteacher makes $22,500 per year. And New York City public schools employ 4,000 administrators at headquarters, while Catholic schools (which teach about a quarter as many students) employ 33.
>
> How do Catholic schools do it? According to *Time* (not exactly a Catholic mouthpiece), "Mostly by practicing and preaching old-fashioned stuff: values, discipline, educational rigor and parental accountability, coupled with minimal bureaucracy." . . . Whatever one's theological position is on Catholicism, the Catholic church holds strong views

on morality, self-discipline, self-control, and high aspira-
tion—all of which are valuable for young students. . . . In
1990, the City University of New York conducted a
national survey that "demonstrates the remarkable educational achievements of the 2.4 million black Roman
Catholics," . . . Black Catholics are 40 percent more likely
to graduate from college than other black Americans . . .
And have 50 percent more households earning more than
$50,000 a year than the rest of the black population.[8]

These statistics demonstrate the tremendous impact on social
justice that a biblically balanced Christianity—both spiritual and
social—has on society. All the governmental bureaucratic welfare programs in the past forty years have not accomplished for
the poor what the Catholic church has already done as a matter
of love for their neighbors.

Private Education on Abortion

We must also educate the public about the human fetus—
privately. The lie that the fetus is a "blob of tissue" has been
successful. To give a better picture of what we are killing, Dr.
John Wilke and Randy Alcorn place pictures of fetuses, both
dead and alive, in their books. They understand that until people
can see with their own eyes that this is a human person, nothing will change (see page 232).

Although I perform hand surgery, I recently placed new
public service announcements in my office. There is a booklet
display on sexual abstinence for teenagers. Many teens and
parents pick up these free booklets. Alongside is a plastic model,
framed in glass with one simple label beneath it: "12-week-old
fetal human." That's one way I'm educating.

The determining factor as to whether a child is practicing
sexual abstinence is not whether they attend church services or
Mass. The rate of sexual promiscuity is just as high inside the
church as outside. What makes the difference is whether or not
the parents take personal involvement in training their children
in values, morals, and expectations. Let's teach them that intercourse is not the only sexual sin—it starts much earlier.

Pastors and schoolteachers can educate by showing fasci-
nating photographs of fetal humans. Some pastors are reluctant

to show pictures in deference to women who have had abortions. They need to remember such women can't ask forgiveness and repent, unless they know what a grievous sin they have committed. A person in denial cannot ask forgiveness. Neither can they heal from the pain until they understand the magnitude of God's full forgiveness.

Frederick Buechner wrote, "Tell her that sin is forgiven because, whether she knows it or not, that's what she wants more than anything else—what all of us want. What on earth do you think you were ordained for?"[9] When the woman realizes the seriousness of the offense, then the forgiveness of God will result in a new appreciation for God's Grace in His Church.

Compassion Is Still True Religion

Victims of abortion violence need compassion. That begins with education about God's view of human life. One thing is sure: His complete forgiveness is available to women who repent. In my view, these women are more victims than murderers.

Unethical doctors—my own colleagues—are happy to earn quick profits for murder. Our society and Planned Parenthood spread the infectious lies of "tissue blobs" and "every child a wanted child" (and if not wanted, then killed). Just as in Germany, medical doctors in America were the impetus for our present abortion policy. Do you know where your doctor stands on the sanctity of life issues? If not, find out. Physicians need educating as well. If your doctor prescribes any pills that cause abortions, speak with the doctor or find another one.

Women who have had abortions need to talk about their painful experiences with other women who can help. Women Exploited By Abortion, Crisis Pregnancy Centers, Sisters for Life, and other organizations provide recovery help for that kind of trauma. When you see the opportunity, reach out with the forgiveness of Christ to those who have been seduced by the deceitfulness of sin.

While we must show the truth, that abortion is killing a human being, we must also show compassion in practical ways to women in their time of distress. Emotional and financial support at this critical time can make a profound difference in a woman's ability to cope with her problem. Francis Schaeffer points out, that for us to say: " 'You must not have an abortion' without being ready to involve ourselves in the problem, is another way of being inhumane."[10]

One study, published in *Reader's Digest,* found that 90 percent of women who had abortions would have carried their children to birth if they had received support.[11] The most common reasons to have an abortion were the inability to continue a career or education, financial pressures, and a lack of understanding from family and friends—especially the father of the child. Yes, men contribute to this sin by sending women off to the abortion clinic with some money to "take care of the problem."

Giving maternity clothing and baby items that are no longer in use are great ways to act in love. Money for ultrasound machines is needed in these clinics so that the pregnant woman can see the living, moving, human being who is growing inside her. It helps her visualize the bumper sticker that reads: "If it's not a baby, you're not pregnant."

It only takes an hour to march in a fundraiser. This brings attention to the holocaust of inhumane abortion while demonstrating compassion. Acting as a phone volunteer at a crisis center requires a little more time. The commitment is certainly worth it if we look at the results.

Almost 40 percent of women who contact a Crisis Pregnancy Center decide *not* to abort their babies.[12] Person to person involvement is the key to long-term change. We won't stop all abortions; sinners will always find ways to kill. But we can help to change public attitudes about the fetal human made in God's image, and about pro-life people themselves, who should act like they are made in God's image.

The Pro-Life Image

The assassination of abortionists does not qualify as acting in God's image, or on His behalf. Violence of any kind does not qualify. Both are to be condemned as sin. The media, and organizations that make huge profits from abortion killings, continue to exploit the occasional violent act by mentally and spiritually deficient persons. These tragedies cast a dark shadow on those who stand for the unborn and God's life priority. This holds true even though not a single case has ever been linked to an organized pro-life group.

Peaceful demonstrations are an excellent way to remind the public that someone still cares for unborn Americans—that life and liberty to all still means *all*. Civil disobedience worked for Martin Luther King, Jr. and our black brothers and sisters. Let us not forget that they have had to pay a heavy price. What price are we willing to pay?

Civil disobedience makes many uncomfortable, because Christians are supposed to obey the law: But keep in mind that natural law supersedes any human law when it comes to human life. Pope John Paul II has reminded us of this point.[13]

The Hebrew women who rescued Jewish newborns in Exodus 1:17-22 gave us an example of peaceful civil disobedience. Trapped between the order of the King of Egypt to kill newborns and the law of God not to murder, they obeyed God rather than man. Even though they had to lie to save the babies, God blessed them for protecting innocent human life. They were not doing the lesser of two evils. They were doing the greatest good—God's priority of life. The New Testament also supports this principle.[14]

Personal Involvement

Myma Shaneyfelt is a 58-year-old who helps women in need, while standing up for God's law. This white-haired grandmother, who is on the Board of Directors of Oregon Right to Life, has "been arrested more than twenty-five times, been pelted with water-filled condoms, and served time in jail."[15]

Not all of us will be willing to endure this treatment for doing what is right—but all of us need to become more active. If each one of us would take one more step, we would make significant progress toward saving the four thousand babies killed every day.

I haven't always acted that way myself. Ten years ago, a patient of mine told me that she'd broken off with her boyfriend until he made headway in straightening out his life. They'd just gotten back together when he was killed in a car accident.

She was pregnant. I wish that I could tell you that I compassionately educated her about the new life she was carrying and guided her to support services. I am still shamed by my response: "This is a tough situation." I don't know what she decided, but I know that I am responsible to God for my silence. I may have contributed to a death.

We are all in process—growing, learning, and seeking God. We need patience with each other and with ourselves. Let's all continue moving toward God's priority of life.

Personal Responses

Some of you have realized for the first time that you have personally contributed to the mass murder of unborn humans. God *does* hold you responsible. Grief *is* appropriate. However, this is *not* a time for despair or self-flagellation. God offers forgiveness to everyone who asks.

The Apostle Paul murdered many innocent humans—Christians. He sought them out and killed them thinking that he was doing the right thing. Then God spoke to Saul. Saul saw the light and Paul the apostle was reborn. Forgiveness, even for murder, is available. In 1 John 1:9 we read, "If we confess our sins He is faithful and just to forgive our sins, and to cleanse us from all unrighteousness." If you have sinned by authorizing the mass murder of millions, ask God for His forgiveness. He is a merciful God. You *will be forgiven.*

You may be a political candidate or politician who has realized for the first time that you have sinned. You have authorized the murder of millions of innocent human beings. Forgiveness is available for the asking. There is also an opportunity to repent with actions to demonstrate your change of mind. Stating that you are *personally* pro-life is *not* enough according to Jesus, James, and Paul. Those words must carry with them action to change the situation.

There must be bold steps to help the helpless—the neighbor in the womb—even at personal cost. Loving my neighbor involves rescuing that neighbor from death—not merely proclaiming that I am opposed to the mass murder. Push for legislation that saves human lives. Your vote with passion can make the difference.

Conclusions

We Christians should accept our responsibility to demonstrate compassion both to women who are in crisis pregnancies, and also victims of abortions. Many will choose to keep their child from dying. Those who have not will experience healing. Person to person involvement will continue to be the most effective way to stop the millions of abortion killings.

Educating other Christians and the public is crucial. The exact words and actions will vary depending upon the individual. When we educate in the classrooms, God must be given equal time. Our Creator expects us to be morally responsible about His unique image in mankind. If we continue to ignore His foundation and priority, the amoral relativism of naturalistic evolution will collapse into anarchy—threatening every human life.

We must make a difference. The future of America and our eternal future as individuals both depend upon a biblical response to this critical issue. George Barna gives us a word of advice about our response: "If you perceive our culture and the Church to be seriously flawed and deficient, and want to be a part of the solution rather than the problem, then you must embrace the role of a revolutionary and start making good things happen today!"[16]

Notes

1. Merton, T., *Seeds of Contemplation* (A New Directions Book, 1972), 271.

2. John 4:1-30.

3. Many of us were taught in public school that the founding fathers were Deists. Rather than accepting someone else's deconstructionist interpretation, I would encourage a look at a more primary source such as direct quotations. I recommend Federer, W.J., *America's God and Country: Encyclopedia of Quotations* (Coppell, TX: Fame Publishing, 1994).

4. *Edwards v. Aguillard*, 482 U.S. 578 (1980).

5. *Stone v. Graham,* 449 U.S. 39 (1980). This decision made it illegal to display the Ten Commandments in a public classroom. It followed the 1962 decision (*Engel v. Vitale*) that prohibited prayer in the schools.

6. Golden, D., "Home-Schooled Pupils are Making Colleges Sit Up and Take Notice," *The Wall Street Journal* (11 February 2000): 1. The article states that Stanford University "accepted 27 percent of homeschool applicants last fall—nearly double it's overall acceptance rate." Discipline and values and personal attention make the difference. Jason Scoggins, Christian homeschool student won a $100,000 scholarship. Part of the reason was his assessment of the public school problem during a seminar debate: "Public schools will never excel because they lack 'intellectual capital' and have to compensate for too many social problems. . . . I know it's said that schools should be agents of socialization. But that's not their role. Their role is to impart knowledge."

7. Schaeffer, F., *The Complete Works of Francis Schaeffer: A Christian Worldview,* vol. 5, A Christian View of the West, 224.

8. Bennett, W.J., *The Devaluing of America: The Fight for Our Culture and Our Children* (Summit Books, 1992; and Focus on the Family Publishing, 1994), 219-220.

9. Buechner, F., *The Final Beast* (New York: Atheneum, 1965), 114-115.

10. Schaeffer, F.A., and C. Everett Koop, *Whatever Happened to the Human Race?* (Fleming H. Revell Co., 1979), 113.

11. Hemanus, "Network of Hope," *Reader's Digest* (November 1991): 132-136.

12. O'Bannon, R.K., "The Modern Crisis Pregnancy Center," *National Right to Life News* (January 2000): 23.

13. Pope John Paul II, *Evangelium Vitae* 1995, 715.

14. Peter and James disobeyed the authorities when they continued to publicly speak out about Jesus Christ in Acts 4:18-20. Perhaps we should take a lesson from them when it comes to school prayers and public speaking about our Savior.

15. "A Powerful Voice for the Unborn," *Medford Mail Tribune* (26 March 1995).

16. Barna, G., *The Second Coming of the Church,* 210.

21.

Victory Is Certain

Whenever I become discouraged, I read the end of the Book. Revelation heralds the reign of the King of Kings and Lord of Lords! We, the bride of Christ, have a *guarantee* from God that *every* wrong will be made right. There will be no more crying, or pain, or dying (Revelation 21:10).

When God's kingdom comes, His will is going to be done. There will be no more need for abortions—not even to save the life of the mother. At that time, pro-choice and pro-life supporters will both win.

Until Then

We don't have to wait until the end for good news. Previously in this book, I've described significant encouraging progress.

The rate of teenage abortions has been declining every year since 1990.[1] The Center for Disease Control in Atlanta reported a decrease in total abortions in 1997—the latest year that statistics are available. It was the lowest rate since 1978![2] Furthermore, one of the factors responsible was "possibly different attitudes about the moral implications of abortion."[3] Coming from a government office, that in itself seems to be a near miracle.

According to Democrats for Life, almost three out of four Americans believe that 90 percent of abortions should be made illegal.[4] Congress twice passed a bill to outlaw partial birth abortions, which the American Medical Association has declared is never needed to save the mother's life. All we need is a morally responsible President who will sign it into law.

Laws banning Partial Birth Abortions have been passed in twenty-seven states (as of 27 December 1999). Although struck down by some State Supreme Courts, this ban was upheld in the 7th U.S. Circuit Court of Appeals for Wisconsin and Illinois. The U.S. Supreme Court is expected to rule on this critical issue this year.[5]

The Unborn Victims of Violence Act (HR 2436) was passed by the U.S. House of Representatives in late 1999. This would establish punishment for persons who injure or kill an unborn child while committing any other federal crime of violence. The Senate is expected to consider it this year.[6]

Be encouraged! Americans are beginning to realize that abortion really does kill a living human being. The progress that has been made can motivate us to be more vocal and actively educate those around us about God's priority of human life.

The Winning Team

Thanks to those of you who have been working to save human lives long before I became involved. Please don't grow weary now. Younger people are seeing the need to teach their peers about the sin of killing a person in the womb. Welcome. This vital issue is worth your time and commitment.

A message to those who are weary: please read the end of the Book. In Revelation, God assures us that He will bring justice and peace on earth. We have His Word on it.

Until then, our order is to be teaching all nations to obey *all* things that He has commanded. To love our neighbor is at the top of the list.

If Christians will return to their Bibles to discover and live out God's principles, I am confident that God will use His Church to stop the abortion holocaust. The Almighty has never required a majority of His people to follow Him in order to bring about His victories. He asks those people who love Him to trust Him and obey Him.

I can envision God's Church rising up in righteousness—putting aside selfish goals to stand for Christ's Holy Kingdom! I see us, God's Church, sacrificing to help our neighbors in need and *proving* to the unbelieving world that God loves all of them. I can see God smiling at us and saying, "Well done my good and faithful servants. You exchanged your priorities for mine: you saved my innocent children from death."

We, the Church, are the team that can make a profound difference! With the Father as our Coach, Jesus as our Captain, and His Holy Spirit as our Power-player, we *are* going to win! Abortion *will* stop. Let's be part of the active roster of team members who will make it happen!

As Henry Wadsworth Longfellow wrote in 1863, in his poem "Christmas Bells,"

> And in despair I bowed my head;
> "There is no peace on earth," I said;
> "For hate is strong
> And mocks the song
> Of peace on earth, good will to men!"
>
> Then pealed the bells more loud and deep,
> "God is not dead; nor doth He sleep!
> The Wrong shall fail,
> The Right prevail,
> With peace on earth, good will to men!"

Final Exam Primer

Question: We have studied history, medicine, law, and theology with Bible passages, including the Parable of the Good Samaritan. These provide strong evidences that help us know how God would vote. Who is our neighbor?

Answer: Our neighbor is any human person in need. Therefore, both the woman in an unwanted pregnancy and the neighbor in her womb are our neighbors.

Question: According to Jesus' teaching, who was a neighbor to the one in need?

Answer: The one who showed compassion.

Question: Having answered correctly, what did Jesus then tell the lawyer to do about it?

Answer: Jesus said, "Go and do the same."

Question: What should we do?

Answer: Go and do the same—demonstrate compassion in action, even at personal cost.

Go ye therefore, and teach all nations, baptizing them in the name of the Father, and of the Son, and of the Holy Spirit, *teaching them* to obey all things whatsoever I have commanded you; and lo, I am with you always, even unto the end of the world (Matt. 28:19-20).

—Jesus

Notes

1. Bennett, W.J., *The Index of Leading Cultural Indicators* (Broadway Books, 1999), 21.

2. The Associated Press, "Abortions fall in 1997 to lowest since 1978," *The Oregonian* (7 January 2000): 1.

3. Ibid.

4. Democrats for Life, accessed 2 February 2000; available from http://www.democratsforlife.org/brochure.html: 1.

5. Andrusko, D., "People Are Tired of the Killing," *National Right to Life News* (January 2000): 13.

6. Ibid., S-3.

Appendix A
Abortion Facts from the Alan Guttmacher Institute (Pro-Choice)

• 49 percent of pregnancies among American women are unintended; one half of these are terminated by abortion.

• In 1996, 1.37 million abortions took place, down from an estimated 1.61 million in 1990. From 1973 through 1996, more than 34 million legal abortions occurred.

• Each year, two out of every 100 women aged fifteen to forty-four have an abortion; 47 percent of them have had at least one previous abortion and 55 percent have had a previous birth.

• An estimated 43 percent of women will have at least one abortion by the time they are 45-years-old.

• Each year, an estimated fifty million abortions occur worldwide. Of these, twenty million procedures are obtained illegally.

• 52 percent of U.S. women obtaining abortions are younger than twenty-five; Women aged twenty to twenty-four obtain 32 percent of all abortions, and teenagers obtain 20 percent.

• Two thirds of all abortions are among never-married women.

• On average, women give at least three reasons for choosing abortion: three fourths say that having a baby would interfere with work, school, or other responsibilities; about two thirds say they cannot afford a child; and one half say they do not want to be a single parent or are having problems with their husband or partner.

• About fourteen thousand women have abortions each year following rape or incest.

• 12 percent of all nonhospital abortion providers offered their patients medical abortion in 1997 (163 providers). [Note: This is abortion by a pill rather than by an operation.]

• 43 percent of nonhospital facilities indicated in 1997 that they would probably provide medical abortions within the next year if the Federal Drug Administration approved mifepristone; 29 percent said they would do so even if mifepristone were not approved, by using methotrexate. [Note: Mifepristone is RU-486. Methotrexate is a cancer and autoimmune suppressive drug currently approved, legal, and readily available.]

• Nine in ten managed care plans routinely cover abortion or provide limited coverage.

Source: http://www.agi-usa.org/pubs/fb_induced_ abortion.html (19 February 2000), rev. February 2000.

Appendix B
President Ronald Reagan:
Sanctity of Human Life Proclamation

America has given a great gift to the world, a gift that drew upon the accumulated wisdom derived from centuries of experiments in self-government, a gift that has irrevocably changed humanity's future. Our gift is twofold: the declaration, as a cardinal principle of all just law, of the God-given, inalienable rights possessed by every human being; and the example of our determination to secure those rights and to defend them against every challenge through the generations. Our declaration and defense of our rights have made us and kept us free and have sent a tide of hope and inspiration around the globe.

One of those rights, as the *Declaration of Independence* affirms so eloquently, is the right to life. In the fifteen years since the Supreme Court's decision in *Roe v. Wade*, however, America's unborn have been denied their right to life. Among the tragic and unspeakable results in the past decade and a half have been the loss of twenty-two million infants before birth; the pressure and anguish of countless women and girls who are driven to abortion; and a cheapening of our respect for the human person and the sanctity of human life.

We are told that we may not interfere with abortion. We are told that we may not "impose our morality" on those who wish to allow or participate in the taking of the life of infants before birth; yet no one calls it "imposing morality" to prohibit the taking of life after people are born. We are told as well that there exists a "right" to end the lives of unborn children; yet no one can explain how such a right can exist in stark contradiction to each person's fundamental right to life.

That right to life belongs equally to babies in the womb, babies born handicapped, and the elderly or infirm. That we have killed the unborn for fifteen years does not nullify this right, nor could any number of killings ever do so. The inalienable right to life is found not only in the *Declaration of Independence* but also in the Constitution that every President is sworn to preserve, protect, and defend. Both the Fifth and Fourteenth Amendments guarantee that no person shall be deprived of life without due process of law.

All medical and scientific evidence increasingly affirms that children before birth share all the basic attributes of human personality—that they are in fact persons. Modern medicine treats unborn children as patients. Yet, as the Supreme Court itself has noted, the decision in *Roe v. Wade* rested upon an earlier state of medical technology. The law of the land in 1988 should recognize all of the medical evidence.

Our nation cannot continue down the path of abortion, so radically at odds with our history, our heritage, and our concepts of justice. This sacred legacy, and the well-being, and the future of our country, demand that protection of the innocent must be guaranteed, and that the personhood of the unborn must be declared and defended throughout our land. In legislation introduced at my request in the First Session of the 100th Congress, I have asked the Legislative branch to declare the "humanity of the unborn child and the compelling interest of birth." This duty to declare on so fundamental a matter falls to the Executive as well. By this Proclamation, I hereby do so.

Now therefore, I, Ronald Reagan, President of the United States, by virtue of the authority invested in me by the Constitution and the laws of the Unites States, do hereby proclaim and declare that the inalienable personhood of every American, from the moment of conception until natural death, and I do proclaim, ordain, and declare that I will take care that the Constitution and laws of the United States are faithfully executed for the protection of America's unborn children. Upon this act, sincerely believed to be an act of justice, warranted by the Constitution, I invoke the considerate judgment of mankind and the gracious favor of Almighty God. I also proclaim Sunday, 17 January 1988, as National Sanctity of Human Life Day. I call upon the citizens of this blessed land to gather on that day in their homes and places of worship to give thanks for the gift of life they enjoy and to reaffirm their commitment to the dignity of every human being and the sanctity of every human life.

In witness whereof, I have hereunto set my hand this fourteenth day of January, in the year of our Lord nineteen hundred and eighty-eight, and of the Independence of the United States of America, the two hundred and twelfth.

Appendix C
The Death of a Mother

This is just one example of an abortionist charged with murder in Arizona. *The Arizona Republic* newspaper of 13 January 1999 carried the following story:

The doctor and clinic administrator accused of allowing a patient to bleed to death after an abortion have been indicted and arrested. Dr. John Biskind, a Cleveland gynecologist who regularly flew to Phoenix to perform abortions at the A-Z Women's Center, and Carol Stuart, were indicted on manslaughter charges Monday in the death of Lou Anne Herron.

> At a news conference late Tuesday, County Attorney Rick Romley said the conduct of Biskind and Stuart in the Herron case was "outrageous." "Anybody can make mistakes. You don't hold people criminally responsible for innocent mistakes," County Attorney Rick Romley said at a news conference late Tuesday. "The conduct by Dr. Biskind is so outrageous, it shocks the conscience. It is our opinion that Lou Anne Heron did not have to die." As for Stewart, Romley said that the administrator was more concerned with the interests of the clinic than with Herron's medical care. Biskind was arrested Tuesday afternoon at his winter home in Scottsdale; Stuart also was arrested Tuesday in the Valley.
>
> An investigation is still pending into a near-abortion at the clinic in which Biskind attempted to abort a fetus that was 37-weeks-old. Biskind later said he believed the fetus was no more than 24 weeks, but when the abortion proved too difficult he ended up delivering a fullterm baby girl.

Romley also said he will expand the investigation to include the clinic's owner, Moshe Hachamovitch, a New York abortion doctor whose other clinics in Texas and New York have had their share of problems.

Employees told police that, based on ultrasound results, they believed Herron was too far along in her pregnancy for a legal abortion. But when they challenged Stuart, they were told by her that Herron was a private patient of Hachamovitch's. On Tuesday, nurse Victoria Kimball, who quit A-Z after Herron's death and who went public with her concerns, said that she was "happy that justice was being served."

Problems began at A-Z in April, when Herron, 33, a mother of two, sought a late-term abortion. Almost immediately after the procedure, employees said, Herron began to have complications and was bleeding heavily. For the next three hours, she complained about being in pain, worried that her legs were numb and cried out for help.

There wasn't a registered nurse on duty, and inexperienced employees said they could not help her. They said they pleaded with Stuart to call 911. Instead, Stuart called in a medical assistant at an affiliated office in Scottsdale and then paged Biskind for guidance. Biskind, who had already left the clinic, reportedly told an employee over the phone, "Well, what do you want me to do? Call 911."

According to the Phoenix police report, Biskind has come to the attention of the Arizona Board of Medical Examiners several times for various complaints. The most severe discipline was a censure in 1996 for gross negligence after the death of another patient, Lisa Bardsley.

Why wasn't this story in the news across our nation? Why have women not been told of these atrocities? The rare fanatics who murder abortionists receive evening television news and front-page coverage. Abortionists who murder innocent women are conspicuously absent from this coverage. Why? Because, with some rare exceptions, the media continues to feed us the propaganda of the pro-choice agenda—kill humans and harm women. The result is tragic. Millions of women at a small but *serious risk—uninformed* women at serious risk. Love and compassion demand honest information.

For other material on deaths and doctors charged with murder, see cases available at http://www.prolifeinfo.org/risk 005.html, accessed 3/28/2000.

Appendix D
Roe V. Wade Memorial Rally Speech
(In Memoriam)
23 January 2000

Two hundred and twenty-four years ago, the founding fathers of this great nation birthed a new kind of government—a government based upon the idea that all people are created by God; and, are therefore, equal.

Today, we stand here unable to recognize that nation which once championed liberty and life equally for all. Twenty-seven years ago, the Supreme Court of this United States declared war upon the unborn of this nation. Thirty-eight million human beings have died. The result of this declaration of war has been an ever-worsening "culture of death." It has permeated our society—it threatens the very existence of America.

We have come to honor these dead who have been killed in this battle. We cannot bring these fellow Americans back to life. We cannot even honor them with gravestones bearing their names. But we, who remain alive, can honor them: we can dedicate ourselves to the great and noble task that remains. The battle against these innocent unborn continues to rage—quietly . . . too quietly. We must not let it rage quietly. We must dedicate ourselves to shouting from every housetop this truth: One person's right to life *cannot* be sacrificed for another's right to happiness through choice.

Our founding fathers did not conceive this nation based upon the personally sovereign right to choose; but upon the right to life and liberty, and then the pursuit of happiness. Liberty of life is the foundational unalienable right! There is no 'liberty' to choose to kill another human. As Abraham Lincoln said, "No one has the right to choose to do what is wrong."

The task before us is great—to abolish this sentence of death upon the unborn—this declaration of war against our unborn neighbors in the womb—those fellow Americans who cry out to us for justice and life! Our task is to return America to the foundational principle of life and liberty *equally* to all—to speak, to persuade, to vote, to act, to march, to pray that 38 million more children may *not* die in vain.

We have no choice but to fight until we win. For if, God forbid, we do not win, this great nation will perish from the earth. But, by His help, there is hope. As we return to and call upon this God of our fathers, that hope will rise up in victory. This battle for life will most certainly be won!

I delivered this speech on Sanctity of Life Day in front of the Capitol building in Salem, Oregon. You probably noticed that the format parallels another speech in memory of the dead, given 137 years ago.

Abraham Lincoln's remarks on another occasion bear repeating at this point:

> Our progress in degeneracy appears to me to be pretty rapid. As a nation we began by declaring that "all men are created equal." We now practically read it "all men are created equal except Negroes." When the Know—Nothings get control, it will read "all men are created equal, except Negroes and foreigners and Catholics." When it comes to this, I shall prefer immigrating to some country where they make no pretense of loving liberty—to Russia for instance, where despotism can be taken pure, and without the base alloy of hypocrisy.[1]

Notes

1. Abraham Lincoln's letter of 24 August 1855 to Joshua F. Speed. John Bartlett, *Bartlett's Familiar Quotations* (Boston: Little, Brown and Co., 1863, 1980), 520.

E.

Appendix E
Dietrich Bonhoeffer:
Christian Martyr

Although I have quoted this pastor previously, I did not have the opportunity to develop his growth process in understanding the role of the Church in the world. These two quotes reveal that we are all in process of maturing—martyrs are made, not born.

G. Leibholz was one of the leaders of the Confessional Church in Germany who knew Pastor Bonhoeffer. In the memoirs to Bonhoeffer's book, *The Cost of Discipleship*, he wrote:

> In the earlier stages of his career Bonhoeffer accepted the traditional Lutheran view that there was a sharp distinction between politics and religion. Gradually, however, he revised his opinion. . . . Bonhoeffer was rightly convinced that it is not only a Christian right but a Christian duty towards God to oppose tyranny, that is, a government which is no longer based on natural law and the law of God. . . . Thus all kinds of secular totalitarianism which force man to cast aside his religious and moral obligations to God and subordinate the laws of justice and morality to the State are incompatible with his conception of life. . . . But to refrain from taking any part in the attempt to overcome the National Socialist régime conflicted too deeply with his view that Christian principles must in some way be translated into human life and that it is the sphere of the material, in state and society, that responsible love has to be manifested. [1]

Dietrich Bonhoeffer was executed in April 1945, by the German government for his resistance against governmental extermination of the Jewish people. In *The Cost of Discipleship*, he explains his change in thinking about the Church and politics.

> Hence, there is certain "political" character involved in the idea of sanctification and it is this character which provides the only basis of the Church's political ethic. The world is the world and the Church the Church, and yet the Word of God must go forth from the Church into all the world, proclaiming that the earth is the Lord's and all that therein is. Herein lies the "political" character of the Church. If we regard sanctification as a purely personal matter which has nothing whatever to do with public life and the visible line of demarcation between the Church and the world, we shall land ourselves inevitably into a confusion between the pious wishes of the religious flesh and the sanctification of the Church . . . the Church is always in the battlefield . . . struggling to prevent the world from becoming the Church and the Church from becoming the world.[2]

Notes

1. Dietrich Bonhoeffer, *The Cost of Discipleship* (New York: MacMillan Publishing Co., 1976), 30.

2. Ibid., 314-315.

F.

Appendix F
The Choice for Abortion: Diane's Story

When I was seventeen, I found myself apart from my family, involved in an unhealthy relationship with a man, and pregnant—which was something I didn't want to think about or deal with. Eventually, though, I did go down to Lovejoy abortion clinic in Portland to make an appointment to have an abortion. I made this decision, because I had no desire to be a mother, and quite honestly, because I was terrified of going through the pain of labor. I just didn't think of it as being wrong.

When I was examined, I was found to be twenty-four weeks or six months pregnant. But, I was assured that although I couldn't have a simple clinical abortion, I could still have one done at a nearby hospital. I agreed. I would have done anything to not be pregnant, and I showed up at the hospital on the scheduled day. I was placed, along with about a dozen other young girls, in a large basement ward which was lined with cots. There, we received a saline injection in our abdomens which was designed to kill our unborn babies and expel their tiny bodies.

I will never be able to forget the sights or sound burned into my mind on that day. After a few hours of labor, we all began to lose our babies. When the girl on my right lost hers, she began shrieking and screamed for the nurses to "get that away from me!" as she crawled backwards up her bed. The girl on my left cried quietly and asked the nurses if hers was a boy or a girl. I felt a violent lurching sensation as the baby slid from my body. It is so sad to me that the only memory I have of my child is that of a small, still huddled form covered in blood, lying on the white sheet of my cot.

When I left the hospital, I determined to put this horrible episode behind me, never thinking about it, never talking about it. My relationship with my boyfriend, never strong, was now almost nonexistent. About this time, some friends of mine introduced me to the pastor of their church. His name was Randy Alcorn. When he saw my precarious living situation, he invited me to come and live with himself, his wife Nanci, and their daughter Karina. While living there, I sensed the extraordinary joy in their existence and I wanted that, too. So I accepted Christ as my Savior. Unfortunately, I was already pregnant again. Knowing that I would never go through a late-term abortion, I decided, with the full love and support of Randy and Nanci, to give my baby up for adoption.

But I was completely unprepared for the feelings of awe that overwhelmed me when I gave birth to a healthy baby boy. I was, however, content with my decision to give him up to a childless Christian couple. Afterwards, I moved out on my own, eager to begin my life as a new believer at Good Shepherd. I became involved with the college-age group, attended a weekly Bible study and weekly functions, as well as church on Sundays. I met a lot of really neat people, including a guy named Rod, who became my boyfriend.

I wish I could end my story there, but I can't. Though I had accepted Jesus as my Savior, I hadn't put my sinful lifestyle behind me. I became deeply involved with Rod and I became pregnant again. If anyone could die of shame, I would be dead. I was so scared everyone would find out and see what a phony Christian and failure I was. I was too scared to tell Rod. I knew he would marry me, but then he would have to tell his parents that I was pregnant. I was so ashamed. My only option seemed to be abortion. So I went down to Lovejoy and had it done, never giving a thought to our baby. I would never tell anyone what I have done. I would go to my grave with this secret. Time passed and my secret remained deeply buried. Eventually, Rod and I married, we had two kids, Josiah and Amy, we bought a house, attended Good Shepherd Church and Growth Groups. But something was wrong.

My hidden sin held God at arms length. I couldn't grow as a believer because I would never let God close to me, afraid he would see me as I really was, sinful and ugly. One day when I had been married for eight years, God decided it was time for me to come to know him better. I felt an intense, growing awareness of the Lord. I was totally overwhelmed by the incredible knowledge of His love. I felt chosen, special, humbled, and loved, not because of what I had or hadn't done, but simply because it was His pleasure to do so. For a week I was compelled to immerse myself in Scripture and constant prayer. And for the first time in my life I fell in love with my God.

At the end of the week I was praying in my room. I prayed, "Lord, I asked you into my life a long time ago, but I never understood about wanting to give something back. I'm willing to die for you." No sooner had the words left my lips when my horrible sin rose up before me. I fell to my face on the carpet and wept as all the years of deceit and hypocrisy paraded before me. I cried even harder as the truth of having murdered my own children slammed into me.

When I went to Rod, I began by saying how sorry I was, over and over. I just couldn't say the words that would tell him that I had taken the life of his first child. If you know Rod, you know how he loves babies. When I finally got the words out, Rod lay his head in his arms at the table. I remember looking at him suffering from this horrible loss, and all I wanted to do was reach out and comfort him. But I couldn't touch him. I felt so unclean, I was the one who had done this to him. When he finally looked up, Rod tried to take my hand in his, but I pulled away. He caught it and held on. Then he asked me to forgive him.

I was stunned. I couldn't say anything. He hadn't responded like I thought he would, like I deserved. Instead, he accepted his responsibility in everything and asked *me* to forgive *him*. We cried, and we asked each other and the Lord to forgive us. The consequences to what I've done are great. I wonder about the children I lost to "choice" and see who they might have looked like in the smiles of Josiah and Amy. Sometimes I think I can almost hear them. But comforting me through it all is the awesome knowledge that the blood of Jesus fully paid for my debt and that He loves me completely.

What you have just read is a true story. Diane told her story at Good Shepherd Community Church on 19 January 1997. She was kind enough to allow me to personally confirm this story, and agreed to allow me to publish it in this book.

Thank you, Diane. Your courage to speak the truth in love will be the key to many women healing from past abortions.

"The one who covers his sins will not prosper, but whoever confesses and forsakes them will have mercy" (Prov. 28:13).

"He that turns away his ear from hearing the law, even his prayer will be an abomination" (Prov. 28:9).

Appendix G
NARAL Roe v. Wade
27th Anniversary Celebration
20 January 2000

Remarks of NARAL President Kate Michelman

Most of America feels good today. Peace and prosperity are ours. The presidential campaign moves along at the edges of our lives—with the same old issues. But, beneath the debate over taxes and health care lies a very different election—and very different choice. At stake in this election—in fact—is the very vision for America—and a woman's place in that vision. At stake are the fundamental freedoms women have been fighting for over the last century. Revolutions that we have won on principle—not power. Revolutions that allow us to walk into this century freer—far freer—than our grandmothers and great-grandmothers ever imagined possible. Women like Elizabeth Cady Stanton, and Susan B. Anthony who marched against the tradition that America's rule belonged to men only. The women who suffered the curses and bullying to give us the right to vote.

Women like Margaret Sanger who awakened the conscience of the nation to the plight of American women enduring the responsibilities of family life without birth control. Women like Rosa Parks who risked their lives to give African-Americans the same rights as other Americans. Women who sat in at the lunch counters—women who led their children into white only schools—women who got knocked down and beaten crossing Selma's bridge. The century's last revolution is our revolution.

NARAL's revolution. The fight to give every woman full reproductive freedom. The fight for women's self determination, dignity and equality. The fight for a woman's right to choose. The fight not yet over.

As I look across this room to all of you who help us carry on our struggle for freedom of choice every day—I ask you to please remember the legacy of those who walked this road before us. Because we are the children of the suffrage movement. We are the children of the birth control movement. We are the children of the civil rights movement. We are the next generations fighting for the same fundamental freedoms for all women.

The pro-choice movement, like other movements, grew from America's small corners as well as its cities. It was a movement of ordinary women and men tired of watching their friends, their sisters, and daughters forced into back alleys—forced to break the law. It was a movement of telephone trees and kitchen meetings and petitions and letter-writing and marches. We came from uniquely different places and situations and backgrounds—all bound by a deep sense of justice. As more and more women suffered and died, it was impossible to understand how this country—so bent on freedom and equality—remained so indifferent. How our political leaders remained so silent. So we brought our cause to a higher place. And we found an ear and a conscience. We found Justice Harry Blackmun.

For all of us—for all women back then—*Roe* was the final judgement we fought and waited for. After so many years of violation and humiliation, the door was finally flung open to full participation in American life. *Roe* is not one-sided. *Roe* is a compromise. *Roe* is neither pro-abortion—nor anti-abortion. But a law that strikes a careful balance between rights and responsibilities. Fundamental to *Roe* is the Constitution's guarantee against government control of our personal lives—against moral judgement from the White House, from the Congress, from the statehouses, from the courts. It is a national promise that women can choose whether or not to have a child. Without condemnation. Without fear. Without judgement. Forever and ever. That's what we believed. We were wrong!

Once again the freedom to choose is at a crossroads. That's what makes the two thousand elections so critical. We can follow the road to a world in which a woman has full citizenship—with complete freedom to choose her own reproductive course. Or we can return to an age of injustice, intolerance, and inequality—an age where politicians and judges force the return of back alley abortions, medical inquisitions, and unwanted pregnancies. An age without *Roe*. Those who would take America back to a time of no choice permeate the fabric of our social and political institutions. They are often self-righteous—intolerant—even hateful. They preach from the pulpit. They sit in county courthouses. They are elected to hospital boards. They picket our clinics. They sit in our state legislatures. They govern our statehouses. And now they control both houses of the United States Congress. They can't reverse *Roe* because they don't control the Supreme Court so they come from the fringes—they attack at the edges—they weaken the foundation. Their target is not so much abortion but women themselves. Punishing the most desperate at first—the most in need. The silent women—young, poor, and isolated. Women forced to choose between enduring an unwanted pregnancy or facing social retribution.

Piece by piece the far right tears at *Roe*. They hollow out the guarantees of *Roe*—the promises. They force women to wait for an abortion. They make them travel hundreds of miles. They humiliate them. They threaten doctors. They criminalize lifesaving procedures. They accommodate violence. The truth is that women today have fewer reproductive rights than their mothers did when *Roe* was decided. The only barrier standing between women and the return to illegal abortion is a pro-choice president. And the next president will determine the balance of the Supreme Court for at least a generation. He will decide whether abortion should be less necessary—or more difficult. The choice in this year's election couldn't be more starkly drawn. One side is pro-choice—and have records to back up their stand. The other side is staunchly anti-choice. They can sing the song of "compassionate conservatism"—but they can't run from their records. One side will not let *Roe* be overturned. The other side owes the far right too much not to. The two "right minded" Justices it takes to reverse *Roe* won't be a presidential prerogative—but a personal IOU. A demand note. Because they well understand that the presidency is for four years—but the Supreme Court is forever.

So, once again *Roe* and the fate of choice hang in the balance. Once again, we're forced to meet the opposition head on. To expose their intent to use the elections to strip women of their reproductive rights. Once again we must wake up a nation of fair-minded people—a nation that believes in freedom and equality—a thoughtful nation that cares deeply for women and their families. NARAL must send the simple message that the freedom to choose is a fundamental American value—right along side freedom of religion—the right to vote and freedom of speech. That choice is about dignity and self-determination—about family—about community. We must make this election a test of values. The value we put on a woman's life. The value we put on her choice to bear a child. The value we put on rearing that child. Values—like freedom and equality—that are not negotiable. Values that become the threshold for our vote. NARAL will carry this message across America. We will make clear the stark choices and consequences of this election. We will find pro-choice voters. We will organize them—and help them spread the word. We will help the last voter to the polls.

We have less than ten months to make bold the choice and the consequence. To convince people of the threat to *Roe*. To convince them of the danger we face in having both an anti-choice president and an anti-choice majority in Congress. Indeed, not since President Hoover have we faced the danger of conservative control of all three branches of government. If NARAL succeeds—if we all succeed—they will come. They will come from small towns and suburbs and big cities. People of every color and every accent. Old men, young women—of all incomes—of all faiths—of both parties. All bound by a deep sense of equality and justice. Bound by the determination to guarantee women full reproductive freedom. To guarantee women an equal place in our society.

So Choice 2000 is more than a campaign for the White House, the Congress and the state legislatures—It's a campaign for all the women and men who have fought so hard before us. A campaign for the tens of thousands of silent women for whom freedom of choice is their only hope. We were all born of this revolution that women began so long ago in America. We draw from their courage. We are emboldened by their determination—by their faith and commitment. Indeed, we are their legacy for the new century. The fight for reproductive freedom is the fight for women's equality and rights. *We* are the people who must carry that torch into the next century. It's that simple.

Source: accessed 24 February 2000; available from NARAL at http://naral.org/publications/press/00jan/012000.html. (No revision date.)

Resources

Pro-Choice Information

Alan Guttmacher Institute: http://www.agi-usa.org/pubs

National Abortion Rights Action League: http://www.naralorg/choice/index.html; 1156 15th Street, NW Suite 700, Washington, D.C. 20005

Planned Parenthood: http://www.plannedparenthood.org; 1-800-829-PPFA

Purchase of Fetal Body Parts for Research: Dr. Alan Fantel http://grants,nih.gov/grants/guide/1994/94.03.11/notice-availability-003.html.

Pro-Life Information

National Life Center: http://www.abortionfacts.com; 1-800-848-LOVE

National Right to Life: http://nrlc.org; 1-(202)-626-8800

Priests for Life: http://www.priestsforlife.org; 1-(888)-PFL-3448

Physicians for Compassionate Care: http://www.pccef.org; 1-(503)-533-8154

Counseling: Pregnancy, Adoption, Post-Abortion

Bethany Christian Services: 1-800-BETHANY (8 A.M.-12 P.M. EST, 7 days per week)

Adoption and Counseling

Birthright: 1-800-550-4900 (24 Hour Pregnancy Hotline)

Catholic Charities: 1-800-CARE-002

National Crisis Pregnancy Helpline: 1-800-521-5530 (24 Hour Hotline)

Project Rachael: 1-800-5WE-CARE (Post-abortion Counseling)

Sisters of Life: 1-(718)-863-2264 (Post-abortion Counseling)

The Nurturing Network: 1-800-TNN-4MOM (M-F, 9-5)

6-week-old embryo (human)

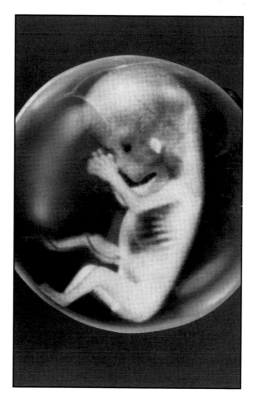

8-week-old fetal human
whose heartbeat can be heard

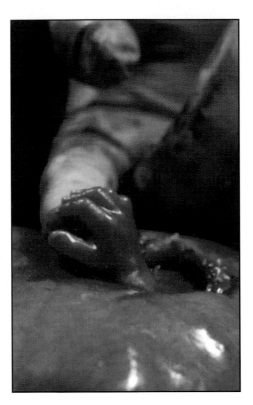

21-week-old fetus receiving a
corrective operation while inside the womb

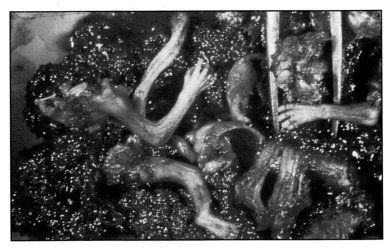

10-week-old fetal abortion
body parts for research

We welcome comments from our readers.
Feel free to write to us at the following
address:

Editorial Department
Huntington House Publishers
P.O. Box 53788
Lafayette, LA 70505

or visit our website at:

www.huntingtonhousebooks.com

═══════════════

More Good Books from Huntington House Publishers & Prescott Press

ABCs of Globalism
A Vigilant Christians Glossary
by Debra Rae

Do you know what organizations are working together to form a new world order? Unlike any book on today's market, the *ABCs of Globalism* is a single volume reference that belongs in every concerned Christian's home. It allows easy access to over one hundred entries spanning a number or fields—religious, economic, educational, environmental, and more. Each item features an up-to-date overview, coupled with a Biblical perspective.

ISBN 1-56384-140-1

Government by Political Spin
by David J. Turell, M.D.

Political Spin has been raised to a fine art in this country. These highly paid "spin doctors" use sound bites and ambiguous rhetoric to, at best, influence opinions, and at worst, completely mislead the public. *Government by Political Spin* clearly describes the giant PR program used by Washington officials to control the information to American citizens and maintain themselves in power.

ISBN 1-56384-172-X

Revelation and the Rapture Unveiled!
by Frank Hart

Revelation and the Rapture Unveiled! is an inductive Bible study of the key prophetic pattern for the fulfillment of events that surround the Second Coming of Jesus Christ and the end of the current age. The information in this book has been presented in a form that is readily understandable for lay people so that they can plainly discern what God has said to us in the Bible through his prophets. The material is profoundly unique in its clear and concise chronology of events, challenging a great deal of contemporay thinking.

ISBN 0-933451-44-X

Are We Living In the End Time?
Prophetic Events Destined to Impact Your World
by Rod Hall

Wars! Famine! Earthquakes! Massive destruction around the globe! Are we living in the end time? Many societal trends and world events are taking shape today. Are the false prophet and antichrist soon to emerge?

ISBN 0-933451-48-2

A Divine Appointment in Washington DC
by James F. Linzey

A spiritual tool on praying in the Spirit and a scholarly tool for the classroom, A Divine Appointment in Washington DC includes testimonials, study guide, index, and a recommended reading list. The author has appeared on television networks such as the Oasis Television Network and Trinity Broadcasting Network.

ISBN 1-56384-169-X

E–vangelism
Sharing the Gospel in Cyberspace
by Andrew Careaga

Cyberspace has become a repository for immense spiritual yearning. The Internet is reshaping the way we work, interact, learn, communicate, and even pray. Provided are ideas for building a website and helpful guides for Christians to find their way around the maze of chat rooms, discussion groups, and bulletin boards found on the Internet.

ISBN 1-56384-160-6

The Deadly Deception
Freemasonry Exposed..
By One of It's Top Leaders
by Jim Shaw and Tom McKenny

This is the story of one man's climb to the top, the top of the "Masonic mountain." A climb that uncovered many "secrets" enveloping the popular fraternal order of Freemasonry. Shaw brings to life the truth about Freemasonry, both good and bad, and for the first ever, reveals the secretive Thirty-Third Degree initiation

ISBN 0-910311-54-4

The Hidden Dangers of the Rainbow
by Constance Cumbey

This nationwide best-seller paved the way for all other books on the subject of the New Age movement. Constance Cumbey's book reflects years of in-depth and extensive research. She clearly demonstrates the movement's supreme purpose: to subvert our Judeo-Christian foundation and create a one-world order through a complex network of occult organizations. Cumbey details how these various organizations are linked together by common mystical experiences. The author discloses who and where the leaders of this movement are and discusses their secret agenda to destroy our way of life.

ISBN 0-910311-03-X

The Coming Collision
Global Law vs. U.S. Liberties
by James L. Hirsen, Ph.D.

Are Americans' rights being abolished by International Bureaucrats? Global activists have wholeheartedly embraced environmental extremism, international governance, radical feminism, and New Age mysticism with the intention of spreading their philosophies worldwide by using the powerful weight of international law. Noted international and constitutional attorney James L. Hirsen says that a small group of international bureaucrats are devising and implementing a system of world governance that is beginning to adversely and irrevocably affect the lives of everyday Americans.

Paperback ISBN 1-56384-157-6
Hardcover ISBN 1-56384-163-0

Cloning of the American Mind
Eradicating Morality Through Education
by B. K. Eakman

Two-thirds of Americans don't care about honor and integrity in the White House. Why? What does Clinton's hair-splitting definitions have to do with the education establishment? Have we become a nation that can no longer judge between right and wrong?

"Parents who do not realize what a propaganda apparatus the public schools have become should read Cloning of the American Mind *by B. K. Eakman."*

—Thomas Sowell, *New York Post*
September 4, 1998

ISBN 1-56384-147-9

The Cookbook:
Health Begins in Him
by Terry Dorian, Ph.D.

The action plan for optimal health and hormone balance! *The Cookbook: Health Begins in Him* offers a dietary regime and food preparation based on both scientific studies and biblical guidelines. Under Dr. Dorian's directions, whole-foods chef Rita M. Thomas has created one hundred and seventy recipes with instructions on:

* *How to prepare breads, pastas, cereals, and waffles with freshly milled flour.*
* *How to prepare desserts that help maintain optimal health.*
* *How to prepare raw vegetable dishes, raw vegetable dressings, cooked vegetables, grain-based casseroles, beans and grains, fermented dishes, and soy foods.*

ISBN 1-56384-127-4

Prayer Without Ceasing ... Breath Prayers
by Kathleen Lewis

Breath Prayers is a profoundly simple means to find mind/body/spirit balance and health. Throughout the Bible we are warned to watch and guard our thoughts. In using *Breath Prayers,* we take the sword of the Holy Spirit, the Word, and breathe it into the body, the Temple of the Holy Spirit: *"For the Word of God is living and powerful, and sharper than any two-edged sword."* (Hebrews 4:12).

ISBN 0-933451-37-7

What Would They Say?
The Founding Fathers on Current Issues
by Glen Gorton

Thomas Jefferson, John Hancock, George Washington — If these men could once again walk through the halls of Congress, surveying the present scene, what would they say? We are being told by the Clinton administration that things like honor and integrity don't matter as long as the rate of inflation is kept down. Our Founding Fathers disagree. They believed that high moral character is an essential ingredient of leadership. Into the heated atmosphere of today's social and political crossfire comes a refreshingly new point of view from -- the Founding Fathers. This is not another analysis of the men and their times, but rather, the penetrating and concise testimony of America's greatest heroes. Herein lies the strength of this 240 page anthology: the Founding Fathers themselves.

What Would They Say? is divided into three parts:

- Part One has quotes under topics covering Character, Patriotism, Federal Power, Crime, Taxes, Education, Gun Control, Welfare, Term Limits, and Religion.
- Part Two gives the reader an animated and personal glimpse into the life of each of the 28 men quoted.
- Part Three contains a copy of the *Declaration of Independence,* the *US Constitution,* and the *Bill of Rights.*

ISBN 1-56384-146-0